W9-BRS-062

THE
Meatless Monday
FAMILY COOKBOOK

This book is dedicated to my children, Matthew, Caroline, and Katherine.
You are my motivation for wanting to live a long and healthy life.
May you always dream big and know that you have what it takes to
accomplish anything you want with passion, hard work, and dedication.

Love you to the moon!

Inspiring | Educating | Creating | Entertaining

Brimming with creative inspiration, how-to projects, and useful information to enrich your everyday life, Quarto Knows is a favorite destination for those pursuing their interests and passions. Visit our site and dig deeper with our books into your area of interest: Quarto Creates, Quarto Cooks, Quarto Homes, Quarto Lives, Quarto Drives, Quarto Explores, Quarto Gifts, or Quarto Kids.

© 2020 Quarto Publishing Group USA Inc.
Text © 2020 Jenn Sebestyen
Photography © 2020 Quarto Publishing Group USA Inc.

First Published in 2020 by Fair Winds Press,
an imprint of The Quarto Group, 100 Cummings Center,
Suite 265-D, Beverly, MA 01915, USA.
T (978) 282-9590 F (978) 283-2742 QuartoKnows.com

All rights reserved. No part of this book may be reproduced in any form without written permission of the copyright owners. All images in this book have been reproduced with the knowledge and prior consent of the artists concerned, and no responsibility is accepted by producer, publisher, or printer for any infringement of copyright or otherwise, arising from the contents of this publication. Every effort has been made to ensure that credits accurately comply with information supplied. We apologize for any inaccuracies that may have occurred and will resolve inaccurate or missing information in a subsequent reprinting of the book.

Fair Winds Press titles are also available at discount for retail, wholesale, promotional, and bulk purchase. For details, contact the Special Sales Manager by email at specialsales@quarto.com or by mail at The Quarto Group, Attn: Special Sales Manager, 100 Cummings Center, Suite 265-D, Beverly, MA 01915, USA.

23 22 21 20   1 2 3 4 5

ISBN: 978-1-59233-905-1

Digital edition published in 2020
eISBN: 978-1-63159-776-3

Library of Congress Cataloging-in-Publication Data

Names: Sebestyen, Jenn, author.
Title: Meatless Monday family cookbook : kid-friendly, plant-based recipes
   [go meatless one day a week?or every day!] / Jenn Sebestyen.
Description: Beverly, MA : Fair Winds Press, 2019. | Includes index.
Identifiers: LCCN 2019033090 (print) | LCCN 2019033091 (ebook) | ISBN
   9781592339051 (trade paperback) | ISBN 9781631597763 (eISBN)
Subjects: LCSH: Vegan cooking. | Cooking (Natural foods) | LCGFT:
   Cookbooks.
Classification: LCC TX837 .S3843 2019 (print) | LCC TX837 (ebook) | DDC
   641.5/6362--dc23
LC record available at https://lccn.loc.gov/2019033090
LC ebook record available at https://lccn.loc.gov/2019033091

Cover and Page Design: Amy Sly
Photography: Alison Bickel Photography
Page Layout: tabula rasa graphic design

Printed in China

The information in this book is for educational purposes only. It is not intended to replace the advice of a physician or medical practitioner. Please see your health-care provider before beginning any new health program.

FSC
www.fsc.org

MIX
Paper from responsible sources
FSC® C016973

THE
Meatless Monday

FAMILY COOKBOOK

Kid-Friendly, Plant-Based Recipes

Go Meatless
One Day a
Week—or
Every Day!

Jenn Sebestyen
FOUNDER OF VEGGIEINSPIRED.COM

QUARRY

Contents

Foreword

———

When I was a Boy Scout during World War II, there was a campaign called Meatless Monday. The idea was to help conserve food for the troops serving in the war. It was a tidy and timely way to package a healthy idea, even if that wasn't the intended goal. It was doable and understandable. Two words said it all perfectly.

Years later, a doctor told me that my cholesterol and blood pressure were way too high and my diet was a big part of it. My father had died of heart disease and when I looked around, I saw these lifestyle diseases everywhere, and they were all self-inflicted. People were putting bad things into their bodies and wreaking havoc on their health.

I had been in the advertising business for years and I asked myself, "Why not sell health instead of products?" However, there was a problem: How do you make moderation positive, fun, and doable without being a nag or a nanny? At the time, the medical community was suggesting cutting meat intake by 15 percent. I did some math and realized that cutting meat by 15 percent meant cutting out meat for just three out of the 21 weekly meals. There was no need to try to do calculations every meal and guess how big 15 percent of a portion was. It was so simple: Skip meat just three meals for one day a week.

People could change their eating habits incrementally and not feel as if they're giving anything up.

So, in 2003, Dr. Bob Lawrence (then the director of the Center for a Livable Future at Johns Hopkins Bloomberg School of Public Health) and I created a modern-day Meatless Monday with the goal of improving the health of both people and the planet. The campaign used the rhythm of the week to its advantage. Friday is pay day, Saturday is play day, and Sunday is pray day. But Monday? That's the day all health breaks loose.

The Monday concept was also backed up with data. More people start diets, begin exercise routines, quit smoking, and search the internet for health information on Mondays than any other day. Surveys show that if you are going to create healthy change, Monday is the day to do it.

It started slowly at first, but then, it really picked up steam. Celebrities like Oprah and Michael Pollan got involved, and famous chefs were featuring special Meatless Monday dishes.

In 2009, Sir Paul McCartney helped us give Meatless Monday a global presence by launching Meat Free Monday in the UK. Today, Meatless Monday is supported by millions of people in over 40 countries and is backed in science and research by the Center for a Livable Future at Johns Hopkins Bloomberg School of Public Health.

I've always said that Meatless Monday works because it gets the idea into the mind before it gets it into the body. Every seven days, you have a chance to start and maintain good habits or break bad ones. This is why I was excited to hear that Jenn Sebestyen was writing a cookbook geared toward the simple practice of creating meatless recipes specifically for Meatless Monday.

Her blog *Veggie Inspired* has been posting amazing recipes for quite some time and she has amassed a nice following. The blog features simple recipes that are healthy and, more importantly, delicious. Who better to write *The Meatless Monday Family Cookbook*? This book provides instructions on making not just meals that are good for you, but also meals that you will crave. This is perfect because giving up meat one day per week shouldn't require giving up flavor.

Jenn has included a friendly introduction that will make getting into a Meatless Monday routine nice and easy. It gives tips on basic kitchen utensils and key ingredients to have on hand.

This Monday, have the whole family help prepare one of the following recipes. Your health and the health of the planet will be grateful.

—Sid Lerner, founder, Meatless Monday global movement

7

Introduction

Hi, friends! Welcome!

If you told me fifteen years ago that I would be eating a plant-based diet today, I would have rolled my eyes. My older brother was, and still is, a vegetarian and—although I respected his decision—I thought it was silly because, you know, the food chain and all!

Growing up, I never thought about how food would affect my body and health. I regularly scarfed down fast-food meals and processed drinks and snacks. I drank milk with every meal and had cheese on nearly everything. Oh, how I loved dairy!

College was more of the same food garbage—beer, pizza, burgers, wings, an occasional salad loaded with cheese and croutons and ranch dressing. The freshman fifteen is real!

Fast forward to being an adult on my own in the working world: I started cooking for myself. Luckily, I have a mom and grandmas that are/were good home cooks, so I had a vague idea of how to do that. Cooking wasn't something I particularly enjoyed, but it was cheaper than eating out all the time and being newly on my own, it was a necessity.

I was still eating meat and dairy at almost every meal. And it wasn't until 2007, when I was pregnant with our first child, that my mindset around food started to change. I knew I needed to eat healthier to sustain the little human I was growing. I cut out a lot of processed foods and sweets (except Lucky Charms . . . hello, pregnancy craving!), and I had drastic aversions to chicken. I had a healthy pregnancy and our son, Matthew, was born happy and healthy.

When Matthew was about three or four months old, I happened across Alicia Silverstone's cookbook, *The Kind Diet*, in the library. I had no idea what the "kind diet" was, and I only knew Alicia Silverstone from *Clueless* and the Aerosmith videos. But I was intrigued. I read it that same night (yes, I read cookbooks like novels), and I vowed never to drink dairy milk again. Knowing that in just a few months, I was going to be making decisions about what foods to feed my young son, I read everything I could about healthy eating. I decided that for me, a plant-based diet was the way to go.

Friends and family were curious and started asking me about the meals I was making. The questions kept coming and in 2012, after quitting my job and having our twin daughters, Caroline and Katherine, I decided to start my blog, *Veggie Inspired*. Originally, it was intended only to be a means to easily share recipes with friends and family and an outlet for me that didn't involve nursing babies or changing diapers around the clock.

I soon found I quite enjoyed creating recipes and blogging. And in the fall of 2014, I posted my now famous recipe for Butternut Squash Mac and Cheese (page 94). It went viral, and I started to believe that people other than me and a few select friends were interested in ditching the meat and dairy as well. My blog has grown exponentially since that time.

Admittedly, my husband and kids do eat meat and dairy—though not often, maybe once a week. Shockingly (*just kidding!*), I am not perfect either. I have been known to nibble a piece of cheese or a sweet treat that may contain eggs if I'm feeling an urge to have it. In this house, we are all about balance. While I do feel that a plant-based diet is the healthiest, and for me I absolutely gravitate toward plant-based foods, I don't stress about my kids' food choices when we eat out or if they are at a party.

My point is this: You don't have to decide today if you want to go meatless forever. In fact, you never have to. But adding more fruits and vegetables to your plate and cutting down on saturated fat and cholesterol can't be a bad thing. I want you to know and believe that eating a plant-based diet can be healthy, satisfying, and totally delicious!

So, who is this book for? This book is for everyone! It's for those who want to incorporate more vegetables in their diet. It's for those who want to make sure their family gets their daily dose of fruits and veggies. It's for those who want to dabble in eating meatless once a week or even just once a month. It's for those who want to stop eating meat altogether. It's for those with dairy intolerance or allergies who need some yummy dairy-free options. It's for those who are already rocking a plant-based diet and are looking for more delicious variety. It's for everyone who loves good food!

It's also for those of all skill-levels in the kitchen. Being a mom to three busy, active kids and a wife to a hard-working husband, I need recipes that are easy and fuss-free. Nothing should take more than an hour, with most recipes averaging around thirty to forty minutes, many just twenty minutes. You'll find tips along the way about how your kids can help you in the kitchen, too!

And let me just tell you a little (embarrassing) story. My very first attempt at cooking was in middle school with a box of mac and cheese. Seems easy enough, right? Well, I somehow missed the part about draining the noodles before adding the milk and cheese powder. Mac and cheese soup, anyone? No? My mom always likes to remind me to this day that I hated to cook when I was younger. So if I can do it, you can do it!

Do you need gluten-free recipes? I've got you covered there, too. Many recipes are already gluten-free. For most others, I've added notes on how to make them gluten-free.

I pride myself on being relatable, approachable, and accessible. If you have any questions for me about the recipes in this book, on my blog, or about meatless meals or ingredients, feel free to contact me around the clock on social media.

CHAPTER 1

Getting Started with Meatless Monday

Why Meatless Monday?

Meatless Monday is a global campaign aimed at helping people reduce their intake of meat and increase their intake of fruits, vegetables, and whole grains. Whether you decide to do this for one day, one week, one month, or forever after is a choice you need to make for yourself. Even one meal per week is a great start if you can't commit to a whole day. This book will give you some great tips about how to get started, how to stock your pantry so a healthy meatless meal is always in reach, and even how to get your kids involved in the process.

There are many different reasons why people choose to go meatless:

- **For Health:** It's no secret that consuming a variety of fruits and vegetables is good for your health. There is no better way to get your daily dose of vitamins, minerals, and fiber. These colorful plants, which are low in saturated fat, also bring us antioxidants and anti-inflammatory properties, which means a possible decreased risk of preventable disease. Are you worried about protein? Don't be! There are plenty of protein-packed foods of the plant variety, such as beans, lentils, quinoa, wild rice, soy, nuts, and seeds. Even fruits and vegetables contain protein!

- **For the Environment:** Ditching the meat could mean a decrease in water consumption and greenhouse gases, which is great for our planet.

- **For Animals:** Obviously, the less meat being consumed, the less animals are needed for butchering.

- **For Economic Reasons:** Pound for pound, beans and whole grains are significantly less expensive than meat. With the added fiber they contain, they'll also fill you up faster and keep you satiated longer, which means you'll need less. Buying fruits and vegetables in season will save you money, as well.

How to Start Your Own Meatless Monday

If you are used to eating meat with nearly every meal, here are two easy ways to ditch it:

#1 Start with flavors and meals you're familiar with and just leave out the meat.

For example: Spaghetti and meatballs. Simply leave out the meatballs. Serve the spaghetti with marinara sauce, garlic bread, and an easy side salad. Or go one step further and add lentils to the sauce instead of meat. Don't expect these meals to have the exact same taste and texture that you're used to. Just appreciate them as the delicious meals they are.

#2 Try new flavors and dishes that you've never had.
If you have no preconceived notions of how something should taste, you may be more willing to forget the fact that there is no meat on your plate.

Whichever option you choose, just start. It really is that easy. Find a recipe you think sounds delicious, buy the ingredients you need, and enjoy it. Don't worry about having a fully stocked pantry and fridge. Take it one day or one meal at a time. There is nothing wrong with going at your own pace.

That being said, it's helpful to know about the ingredients and kitchen tools you're likely to use most often for your meatless meals.

Pantry and Kitchen Essentials

A well-stocked kitchen is essential to getting meals on the table quickly and without frustration. Many of these items may be familiar to you, but you might be surprised at their versatility. A few others may be new to you. For the most part, they are easy to find, and I promise you'll get good use out of them.

Don't feel that you must have all these items stocked all at once. Over time, you'll build up your pantry, spices, and nonperishables. As you become comfortable cooking with these ingredients, you'll find that many can be interchanged or substituted to suit your family's tastes. If you have a few items on hand from each category, you'll be able to make delicious, nutritious meals.

LEGUMES

Legumes are full of healthy plant-based protein, and they're low in fat. They're inexpensive and incredibly versatile. I have a few bags of dried beans in my pantry, but I mostly rely on canned for convenience. Here are a few favorite legumes:

- **Canned:** black beans, cannellini beans, chickpeas, kidney beans, and pinto beans
- **Dried:** brown/green lentils, and red lentils
- **Refrigerated:** firm or extra-firm tofu (which is made from soybeans)
- **Frozen:** shelled edamame

This cookbook may be all about dinners, but I use black beans, chickpeas, and silken tofu in desserts, too! Check out my blog at www.veggieinspired.com for some sweet recipes featuring legumes.

GRAINS

Full of fiber and protein, whole grains keep us feeling satiated. They bring loads of different textures, and there are quite a few gluten-free options. They're just as great for breakfast as they are for dinner. Here are a few preferred grains:

- **Brown Rice:** This might come as a surprise, but I usually buy the quick-cook kind. It can be ready in just 10 to 15 minutes—which is a huge time-saver—and the nutrient difference between quick-cook and regular brown rice is minimal.
- **Jasmine Rice:** Commonly used in Asian cooking, but because it cooks in just 15 to 20 minutes, I use it often in all kinds of dishes. It has a lovely subtle flavor of its own, and for me, that makes it a better choice than bland white rice.
- **Oats:** Most people only eat oats for breakfast, but they are quite versatile and can be used in so many ways. Savory oats are delicious and can make a quick lunch. I use whole rolled oats most often as a binder in veggie burgers.
- **Quinoa:** Quinoa is naturally gluten-free and a complete protein. Bonus: It cooks in just 15 to 20 minutes.

PASTA

Pasta can be made from grains, beans, or even vegetables and it comes in a variety of shapes and sizes to suit almost any dish. There are plenty of gluten-free varieties available today as well. And here's what I know—add noodles to just about any dish and it just got a whole lot more kid-friendly. Kids love noodles! Here are some of our favorite pasta shapes:

- Macaroni
- Penne
- Rigatoni
- Rotini
- Shells
- Spaghetti
- Ziti

NUTS AND SEEDS

Raw nuts and seeds contain healthy fats and protein. They are great for snacking and adding crunch to meals. They can even be used to create creamy sauces. Nut and seed butters are wonderful on toast or crackers, and they can be stirred into sauces for depth of flavor. Look for nut butters that are just ground nuts and, maybe, salt. Here are a few favorite nuts and seeds:

- **Raw Nuts:** almonds, cashews, hazelnuts, pecans, and walnuts
- **Seeds:** hemp seeds, ground flax seeds, sesame seeds, and shelled pumpkin seeds
- **Nut Butters:** almond butter and natural peanut butter

We also love cashew butter and chia seeds. I use those mostly for baking, so you won't find them in this book.

DRIED SPICES AND HERBS

Welcome to the easiest and most affordable way to add flavor to your recipes. I love fresh herbs to finish a dish, but it's the dried herbs and spices that I use the most. Dried herbs and spices won't spoil, but you won't be getting their full flavor potential if you haven't replaced them in a few years. Slowly start to replace the old outdated ones with new and you'll taste the difference. I keep more dried herbs and spices in my pantry than I can count. Here are a few staples:

- Basil
- Black Pepper
- Chili Powder
- Cinnamon
- Cumin
- Garlic Powder

- Ginger
- Himalayan Pink Salt
- Italian Seasoning
- Nutmeg
- Onion Powder
- Oregano
- Paprika
- Rosemary
- Sage
- Smoked Paprika
- Thyme
- Turmeric
- Crushed Red Pepper Flakes
- Yellow Curry Powder

A note about Himalayan pink salt: I nearly always use this type of salt. It contains trace minerals that table salt doesn't have, and I prefer the flavor. I find it less "salty," and it does have a bit less sodium than table salt, as well. For the recipes in this book, use the salt that you prefer.

Although I list specific amounts for every ingredient in these recipes, I encourage you to taste before serving and adjust the seasoning to your liking. We all have different palates and there is nothing wrong with making a dish your own.

OILS

Due to their high fat content, oil brings flavor, richness, and moisture. Lately, it seems that more and more people are trying to eliminate oil from their diets. I'll admit, I tend cook more and more without any added oils. For the purposes of this book, I wanted as much flavor as possible, so I do use oil in these recipes. If you want to go oil-free, to sauté, try using ¼ cup (60 ml) of water or broth and add more as needed to prevent sticking. If you are using oil, here are a few I use most often:

- **High-heat Cooking, Panfrying, or Roasting:** avocado oil, coconut oil (also in spray), and peanut oil
- **Sauces and Dressings:** extra-virgin olive oil
- **Sautéing:** olive oil
- **Asian-Inspired Dishes:** sesame oil (for finishing)

CONDIMENTS AND FLAVORINGS

These are the ingredients that are going to take your dishes from good to great. A little goes a long way and sometimes just a spoonful or two is all you need. You may not always detect them in the finished dish, but they will bring depth of flavor and add that extra something.

- **Vinegars:** Raw apple cider vinegar, balsamic vinegar, red wine vinegar, rice vinegar, and white wine vinegar

- **Coconut Aminos (gluten-free and soy-free), Tamari (gluten-free), and Soy Sauce:** These are all basically interchangeable. I prefer the taste of coconut aminos and tamari as I find them a bit less salty.

- **Lemon and Lime Juice:** A squeeze of fresh lemon or lime juice to finish a dish can make all the difference! I always think fresh is best but bottled 100% juice is great in a pinch.

- **Mellow White Miso Paste:** Miso is fermented soybean paste. Generally, the soybeans are combined with grains, such as rice or barley. If you are gluten-free, you will need to check the label to see which kind of grains are used. There are several kinds of miso on the market, but the one I use nearly exclusively is the mellow white miso paste by Miso Master. Like the name says, the flavor is mellow, so it's more versatile and can easily be added to a variety of dishes. It's also certified gluten-free. It may be a bit trickier to find this ingredient than the others, but trust me, it's so worth it! It won't go to waste—I use it in quite a few recipes in this book and there really is no substitute. It will keep in the fridge almost indefinitely, so no worries about it going bad before you have a chance to use. Find it, buy it, love it!

- **Nutritional Yeast:** This is a deactivated yeast. Although it's technically made from the same type of yeast, it is not the same as brewer's yeast or baker's yeast. Most often you'll find fortified nutritional yeast, which is a complete protein and contains vitamins and minerals. Most brands contain vitamin B12, which is sometimes hard to get enough of on a plant-based diet. It should be noted that even meat eaters are at risk for B12 deficiency, so it's a wonderful product to add to every type diet. The taste is savory and a little nutty. Some think it has a cheesy flavor, and while I do think it plays nicely in "cheesy" sauces, it definitely doesn't taste like cheese on its own. It can take a little getting used to, but once you do, it can become a crave-able taste. I use it sparingly throughout this book, and most times, I mark it as optional. Most stores these days are carrying it, so it shouldn't be too hard to find.

- **Sriracha or Hot Sauce:** A few dashes go a long way and can really kick up the flavor of a dish. Sriracha is big on chili heat and flavor; typical hot sauce is more vinegar-forward. Both are delicious. They may not be very kid-friendly, depending on your child's tastes. My son used to eat salsa by the spoonful when he was just a toddler, so I think the term kid-friendly is relative. These sauces are generally added just before serving, so if you're worried about the heat level for kids, simply serve them their portion before adding any hot sauce.

- **Tahini:** Tahini is sesame seed paste with a texture like peanut butter; it has a savory, slightly nutty taste that can be a bit bitter but is easily balanced with other ingredients, such as vinegar and pure maple syrup. Every brand is a bit different in terms of bitterness, so you may have to try a few to see what you prefer. I love making sauces with tahini as it adds so much flavor.

- **Worcestershire Sauce:** Look for one that says vegan on the label to avoid anchovies. There are several plant-based brands available these days. Worcestershire sauce has an unmistakable savory, yet sweet and tangy, taste that is very hard to emulate with other ingredients.

OTHER PANTRY STAPLES

There shouldn't be too many unfamiliar ingredients here. I always keep these stocked up:

- **Canned Tomato Products:** Crushed, diced, sauce, fire-roasted, paste—basically, if it's a canned tomato product, it's useful!

- **Full-fat Coconut Milk:** This is great for adding creaminess to a dish where the coconut flavor is welcome.

- **Lite Coconut Milk:** This is not quite as creamy as full-fat coconut milk, but still richer than most other plant milks. It is my go-to plant milk for cooking as it doesn't have any noticeable coconut flavor, but still lends a creamy richness.

- **Mayo:** I use an egg-free mayo to keep plant-based. There are several on the market today but use what you're comfortable with.

- **Pure Maple Syrup:** This is my sweetener of choice. It's unrefined, sweet, and delicious. It helps to balance acidity in sauces and dressings. Of course, it's great in baking and desserts, too!

- **Roasted Red Peppers:** These are so much easier and quicker than roasting your own. And they bring a ton of flavor.

- **Salsa:** Allllll the salsa! We love salsa, and eat chips and salsa on the regular, but salsa is not just for dipping those chips. It brings great flavor—spicy or mild—to many recipes. My favorite is a traditional spicy tomato-based salsa, but there is certainly a time and place for smoky roasted salsa, salsa verde, and fruit-based salsa as well.

- **Tortillas**: Our family prefers flour tortillas, but corn tortillas are great for a gluten-free option. They're perfect for traditional wraps, quesadillas, enchiladas, and burritos, but you can stuff just about anything, including leftovers, in a tortilla and transform it into something tasty. I often add sandwich ingredients to a tortilla, roll it up, and slice it into bite-size pieces for the kids' lunch boxes.

Kitchen Tools

I don't think you need a ton of gadgets in your kitchen to be successful, but it definitely helps to cut down on prep and cooking time when you have a few key pieces. Here are a few items that I couldn't live without:

- **Casserole Dishes:** I have a few of these. I think it's a great start to have one square (8- × 8-inch or 9- × 9-inch [20 × 20 cm or 23 × 23 cm]) and one rectangular (9- × 13-inch [20 × 33 cm]) dish.

- **Chef's Knife:** This is my #1 favorite kitchen item. If you are cooking from this book, you're going to be chopping lots of vegetables. Nothing does it better than a sharp chef's knife. There are plenty of gadgets available these days for specialty uses—a garlic press, apple corer, citrus peeler, herb scissors, and avocado peeler, just to name a few. If you like those things, go for it—but a sharp chef's knife can do all that and more.

- **Cutting Boards:** If you're going to be chopping, you need a cutting board. It's nice to have a variety of sizes, but you'll want at least one large one. Although you won't find any in this book, if you eat meat, I suggest you have one to use specifically for meat and one specifically for fruits, vegetables, tofu, and all other plant foods.

- **Food Processor:** This is likely my most used kitchen appliance. Most of them come with a variety of blade options. You can make all the sauce, pesto, nut butter, and hummus you desire, and you can also shred, grate, and thinly slice vegetables. It's wonderful for pulsing and combining ingredients for veggie burgers and patties. You can even use it to make dairy-free ice cream!

- **High-Speed Blender:** High-speed blenders are expensive, but I think they're worth it. I use mine multiple times per week and sometimes multiple times per day. It's perfect for smoothies, soups, and sauces. Most times, a regular blender is fine, but dairy-free sauces often use nuts as a base and there really is no comparison to what a high-speed blender can do in these instances. You can find them refurbished and just as good as new, but much less expensive.

- **Immersion Blender:** This one is not a necessity, but it's inexpensive and I use mine quite often. It's so much easier to purée a soup right in the pot than to have to carefully transfer hot liquid to a traditional blender and then transfer it back. Plus, it's easier to clean than a large blender.

- **Measuring Cups and Spoons:** If you plan to follow a recipe correctly, you'll need these. Liquid and dry ingredients are measured differently, so you'll need both.

- **Mixing Bowls:** Mixing bowls are not just for stirring batter. I use my bowls to toss chopped vegetables with oil and spices before roasting, mixing ingredients for veggie burgers, mashing chickpeas for a sandwich filling, and more. Heck, sometimes I even make myself a big salad for lunch and I eat it out of a large mixing bowl!

- **Parchment Paper:** Parchment paper is great for lining baking sheets to prevent sticking. It means less oil is needed and it certainly makes for easier clean up, too. You can even buy them precut in rectangles that will fit your baking sheet perfectly. They cost more but save time!

- **Potato Masher:** This is not just for potatoes! Although I do use mine to mash potatoes, I use it most often to mash beans for burgers, sandwich fillings, tacos, etc. It's an inexpensive and handy tool you may find you use more often than you expected. Bonus: It's a tool kids can use easily and safely.

- **Pots, Pans, and Skillets:** This is probably a given and, if you've ever cooked before, you're likely to already have them. At minimum, it's nice to have a big soup pot with lid (which could double as a pasta pot), a medium-size pot with lid for sauces and grains, a sauté pan, and a large, deep skillet with lid. If you plan on cooking a lot, having a variety of sizes of each is great and makes it easier to prepare several components of a dish at the same time.

- **Rimmed Baking Sheets:** Of course, these are great for baking, but I also use my rimmed baking sheets all the time for roasting vegetables, cooking veggie burgers, toasting nuts, etc. I think two large ones are ideal. I often use them both at the same time as overcrowding the pan when roasting is a no-no.

- **Salad Spinner:** A salad spinner makes quick and easy work of washing greens.

Bonus: My kids love to operate this thing! They actually fight over who gets to spin it and challenge each other to see who gets the most water out of the greens. If that's not worth the buy, I don't know what is!

· **Spatulas and Spoons:** Again, these are probably things you already have, but worth mentioning because you need a few. I like to have silicone spatulas and wooden spoons on hand because sometimes I'm using several at the same time.

· **Strainers:** A large strainer for draining pasta is a must. A smaller fine-mesh strainer is great for draining and rinsing canned beans, draining canned fruit, and rinsing grains and berries. I like to have a variety of mesh strainers on hand, but one medium-size strainer will likely get all the work done.

· **Vegetable Peeler:** There just is no easier way to peel vegetables, and it's a great tool for older kids to use.

· **Whisks:** A whisk is the best tool for making sauces come together. I like having a big balloon whisk to use in pots, a small balloon whisk to use in bowls or jars, and a flat whisk to get in the corners of pots and pans. A flat whisk is also great for sauces with chunkier ingredients.

Getting the Kids Involved

It's no secret that vegetables aren't the top choice of most kids. So, how are you supposed to get your kids on board with your veggie-heavy Meatless Monday plan? I have a few tips and tricks that have worked for our family, and I'm sure some of them will work for you, too.

START THEM YOUNG

The number one piece of advice I can give is to start your kids on a healthy diet as early as possible. We all fall into comfortable habits, especially kids, so make yours a habit of eating nutritious food. Even if they only take one bite, that's okay! It's getting them used to the taste and texture and the habit of trying something new.

My kids were all great eaters when they were toddlers, trying and loving just about anything we put in front of them. It wasn't until they went to school and started noticing what other kids were eating that they started getting a bit pickier. These days, I let my kids buy school lunch usually once a week and they are free to choose whatever they want. Although they love junk food as much as the next kid, they often choose

the salad option because they have developed a true love of most vegetables. Do yourself a favor and steer clear of traditional "kid foods" for as long as possible.

OFFER VARIETY

I try to offer at least two different vegetables with each meal. I encourage my kids to take both, but if they only take one, that's okay with me. Don't give them the option of choosing none. "Do you want broccoli or green beans or both?" There are only three correct answers to that question, and "none" is not one of them.

DON'T SHY AWAY FROM FLAVOR

It's true that tiny taste buds might not be able to handle as much spice and seasoning as adults, but that doesn't mean they need completely bland food either. No one wants to eat bland boring vegetables, adults and kids alike!

CHANGE UP THE TEXTURE

Texture is a huge issue for most people, especially kids. If your kids don't like baked potatoes, try cutting them into bite-size pieces and roasting them, or mashing them, or dicing them and adding them to soups. Same goes for any vegetable or new food—change up the way you serve it and that may make all the difference.

I prefer broccoli roasted with a little olive oil and salt. My son and youngest daughter love it this way, too. But my oldest daughter doesn't care for it; she prefers hers steamed just until tender with absolutely nothing on it. Who would have thought? You just never know, so don't make assumptions about what they will like.

LET YOUR KIDS PICK THE MEAL

Give your child a few recipes to choose from and let them decide which one sounds best. If you have multiple kids, like we do, assign each child their own day to choose.

TAKE THEM GROCERY SHOPPING WITH YOU

Trust me, I know it seems like more work to have your kids with you as you shop but try making it a game. Ask them to pick out one new vegetable to try each time. Kids are more likely to try something new when it is their idea.

If you can find a farmers' market in your area, these are wonderful places to discover local fruits and vegetables. Often, the farmers have samples set out to try or they will let you sample something if you ask. You might hear a wonderful story about how it was grown, too, which is another fantastic way to get kids interested.

ASK YOUR KIDS TO HELP YOU COOK

Children love to imitate adults, so bring them in the kitchen with you. If this seems like a messy, potentially unsafe situation, you're not alone. But the truth is, messes can be cleaned—get the kids to help you with this, too! There are plenty of age-appropriate cooking skills that can be handed off to the kids. My kids love to do all of the following: help set the table; grab ingredients out of the fridge or pantry; wash vegetables; measure out ingredients; stir; peel vegetables; chop vegetables (older kids); mash beans or potatoes; use the strainers to rinse beans, grains, and berries. And they really love to use the salad spinner. Of course, you need to remain close by, ensure they are using any kitchen tools correctly, and have them stay away from hot or sharp surfaces, but kids can do so much more than they are often given credit for.

Look for my "Kids in the Kitchen" tips throughout the book for ways your kids can help to make the recipes. Of course, every child is different and has a different skill level. Just because my eleven-year old is allowed to chop vegetables and use the stove, doesn't mean yours should. But you can, and should, teach your child proper knife and stove safety so that you can all enjoy time cooking together.

Only you know what your child can handle. Always remain close by to supervise and help, if needed.

SET A GOOD EXAMPLE

Bottom line, if you want your kids to branch out and try new things, make sure they see you preparing, eating, and enjoying new foods, too.

CHAPTER 2

Hearty Soups

I make soup all year round—brothy soups, chunky soups, vegetable soups, bean soups, noodle soups, winter soups, summer soups . . . I love them all. Soup is a great way to use up ingredients that are hanging out in the back of your fridge. I also find soup is a great way to pack in a lot of nutrition from a variety of vegetables that my kids might otherwise not want to eat. The soups in this chapter are my go-to recipes for comforting, filling, healthy, and flavorful bowls of goodness.

Easy Black Bean Soup

This quick and easy soup needs just nine ingredients and thirty minutes. Packed with healthy plant-based protein, vegetables, and spices, this cozy meal is perfect for a weeknight.

2 tablespoons (28 ml) olive oil

1 yellow onion, diced

2 cloves garlic, minced

1 red bell pepper, diced

1 teaspoon cumin

½ teaspoon dried oregano

½ teaspoon smoked paprika

½ teaspoon salt, or to taste

3 cans (15 ounces, or 425 g each) black beans, rinsed and drained (or 4 cups [688 g] cooked beans)

1 can (14.5 ounces, or 410 g) diced tomatoes

3-4 cups (700–946 ml) low-sodium vegetable broth

FOR SERVING (OPTIONAL):

Diced avocado

Sliced scallion

Chopped tomato

Fresh lime juice

Hot pepper sauce

Crushed tortilla chips

Yield: 4 to 6 servings

In a soup pot over medium heat, heat the olive oil and sauté the onion for 5 to 6 minutes until softened and translucent. Add the garlic and bell pepper and sauté for 2 to 3 minutes. Add the cumin, oregano, smoked paprika, and salt and sauté for another 1 to 2 minutes until the spices are fragrant.

Add the black beans, tomatoes, and 3 cups (700 ml) of vegetable broth. You can add more broth later if you like a thinner soup. Bring to a boil. Reduce the heat to low and simmer for 15 to 20 minutes.

Using an immersion blender, purée half of the soup. Alternatively, you can carefully transfer half of the soup to a blender, purée, and add it back to the pot. Add the other cup (235 ml) of broth if you like a thinner soup.

Serve hot with the toppings of your choice.

Add It!

My kids love this soup with macaroni noodles!

Kids in the Kitchen

Have your kids measure out the spices and rinse the beans with a mesh strainer.

Cauliflower Wild Rice Soup

This soup isn't going to win any prizes for its beauty, but it's flavorful and hearty. The wild rice, a complete protein, lends a wonderful chewy texture. Cauliflower is low in calories and is an excellent source of many vitamins and minerals. This soup takes a bit longer to make because of the wild rice, but it's so worth it for the flavor and texture, and most of the time involved is hands off.

2 tablespoons (28 ml) olive oil

1 yellow onion, diced

2 ribs celery, diced

3 carrots, peeled and diced

2 tablespoons (28 ml) white wine vinegar

2 cups (200 g) chopped cauliflower

6 cups (1.4 L) low-sodium vegetable broth

2 teaspoons dried thyme

2 teaspoons dried sage

1 teaspoon dried rosemary

1 teaspoon basil

½ teaspoon salt

¼ teaspoon black pepper

1 cup (160 g) uncooked wild rice mix

1 cup (235 ml) lite coconut milk or unsweetened plain almond milk

Yield: 6 servings

Heat the olive oil in a big soup pot over medium-high heat. Add the onion and sauté for 4 to 5 minutes until soft and translucent. Add the celery and carrots and sauté for 4 to 5 minutes until starting to soften. Add the white wine vinegar and stir until mostly evaporated. Add the cauliflower, vegetable broth, thyme, sage, rosemary, basil, salt, and pepper. Increase the heat to bring to a boil and then reduce the heat to simmer for 10 minutes or until the cauliflower is tender.

Using an immersion blender, purée about half of the soup. Alternatively, you can carefully transfer half of the soup to a blender, blend until smooth, and then pour it back in the pot.

Add the wild rice mix and coconut milk. Increase the heat to bring the soup back to a boil and then reduce to medium-low to simmer for 35 to 45 minutes until the rice is tender, stirring frequently to ensure the rice doesn't stick to the bottom of the pot.

Kids in the Kitchen

Smaller kids can help by pulling the florets off the cauliflower and peeling the carrots. Older kids can help by chopping vegetables.

Creamy Tomato Soup with Orzo

Tomato soup is a staple. It's great as a combo with sandwiches or salads, but this version is hearty enough to stand alone. White beans add fiber and protein, but they are puréed into the soup so no one will ever know they're in there. Orzo pasta adds bulk and a kid-friendly vibe.

2 tablespoons (28 ml) olive oil

1 sweet onion, diced

2 cloves garlic, minced

1 teaspoon cumin

2 teaspoons dried basil

1 can (15 ounces, or 425 g) cannellini beans (white kidney beans), drained and rinsed

1 can (28 ounces, or 785 g) crushed tomatoes

2 tablespoons balsamic vinegar

1 teaspoon salt, or to taste

3 cups (700 ml) low-sodium vegetable broth, divided

½ cup (84 g) uncooked orzo

Yield: 4 servings

In a large soup pot, heat the olive oil over medium-high heat. Add the onion and sauté for 4 to 5 minutes until soft and translucent. Add the garlic, cumin, and basil. Sauté for 1 minute until fragrant.

Add the cannellini beans, crushed tomatoes, balsamic vinegar, salt, and 2 cups (475 ml) of vegetable broth. Raise the heat to high to bring to a boil and then reduce the heat to medium-low and simmer for 10 minutes.

Using an immersion blender, purée the soup until smooth. Alternatively, you can carefully transfer the soup to a blender, in batches if necessary, blend until smooth, and return it to the soup pot.

Add the ½ cup (about 84 g) of orzo and remaining 1 cup (235 ml) of vegetable broth. Stir. Bring the soup back to a boil over high heat and then reduce to a simmer again over medium-low heat and simmer for 10 to 12 minutes until the orzo is tender, stirring occasionally to prevent sticking.

Serving Suggestion
Serve with garlic bread or a slice of crusty bread.

Easy Minestrone with Macaroni Noodles

This soup is a modified version of a soup that my mom made all the time when I was growing up. It's hearty and flavorful and reminds me of childhood, although a bit healthier. Because it's made with nearly all staple ingredients, it's one of my go-to meals. I like to chop the kale into very small pieces to make it easier for the kids to eat.

1 tablespoon (15 ml) olive oil

½ sweet onion, peeled and diced

2 cloves garlic, peeled and minced

1 package (16 ounces, or 455 g) frozen mixed vegetables

1 can (28 ounces, or 785 g) crushed tomatoes

4 cups (946 ml) low-sodium vegetable broth

1 tablespoon (1 g) dried parsley

1 teaspoon dried oregano

½ teaspoon dried thyme

1 teaspoon salt, or to taste

⅛ teaspoon black pepper, or to taste

1 can (15 ounces, or 425 g) canned red kidney beans, rinsed and drained (or 1½ cups [266 g] cooked beans)

1 cup (67 g) chopped kale leaves

2 cups (280 g) cooked macaroni noodles (gluten-free, if desired)

1 tablespoon (4 g) nutritional yeast (optional)

Yield: 4 servings

Heat the olive oil in a soup pot over medium heat. Sauté the onion and garlic for 4 to 5 minutes until translucent and soft. Add the frozen vegetables, crushed tomatoes, vegetable broth, parsley, oregano, thyme, salt, and pepper. Simmer for 20 minutes to allow the vegetables to become tender and the flavors to mingle.

Add the kidney beans, kale, and noodles and simmer for another 2 to 3 minutes to warm through. Take off the heat. Add the nutritional yeast, if using, and stir.

Swap It!

Use spinach instead of kale, if you prefer.

Miso Soup with Shiitake Mushrooms and Ramen Noodles

This soup is everything: cozy, comforting, healthy, easy, and so delicious. Recipe testers fell in love with this recipe! I love making this soup when I feel myself coming down with a cold. It's soothing! My kids tend to pick around the mushrooms, but that's okay because it means more for me.

1 tablespoon (15 ml) olive oil, plus more if needed

2 cloves garlic, minced

1-inch (2.5 cm) piece fresh ginger, peeled and minced

8 ounces (225 g) shiitake mushrooms, stems removed, caps thinly sliced

4 tablespoons (64 g) mellow white miso paste

2 tablespoons (28 ml) tamari (gluten-free, if desired)

½ teaspoon turmeric

8 cups (1.9 L) low-sodium vegetable broth

6 ounces (170 g) instant ramen noodles (Use 4 ounces [115 g] thin rice noodles for gluten-free.)

3 collard leaves or lacinato kale, chiffonade

Sriracha or hot pepper sauce (optional)

Yield: 4 to 6 servings

Heat the olive oil in a large soup pot over medium heat. Add the garlic and ginger and sauté for 1 minute until fragrant.

Add the mushrooms, stir, and sauté for 5 to 6 minutes. The mushrooms should give off some of their own liquid, but if the pot seems too dry, add an additional tablespoon (15 ml) of olive oil or a few tablespoons (60 ml) of vegetable broth.

Add the miso, tamari, and turmeric and stir to coat the mushrooms. Add the vegetable broth, raise the heat to bring to a boil, and then reduce the heat to low and simmer for 15 minutes.

Add the instant ramen noodles and collard leaves and simmer for another 3 to 5 minutes until the noodles are tender.

Serve with a few dashes of sriracha in each bowl, if desired.

Kids in the Kitchen

Have your kids pull the stems off the mushrooms.

Creamy Vegetable Noodle Soup

This thick and creamy soup reminds me a bit of potpie filling, but in soup form. The small ditalini pasta rings are the same size as the diced vegetables, making it easy for kids to scoop up a bit of everything in one bite. Made with no cream, not even homemade cashew cream, you won't believe how creamy it is. You'll be heading back for seconds in no time.

2 tablespoons (28 ml) olive oil

1 yellow onion, diced

3 carrots, peeled and diced

2 ribs celery, diced

1 red bell pepper, seeded and diced

1 tablespoon (1 g) dried parsley

1 teaspoon dried basil

1 teaspoon dried thyme

½ teaspoon dried dill

1¼ teaspoons salt, or to taste

¼ cup (32 g) all-purpose flour

2 cups (475 ml) unsweetened almond milk or milk of choice, divided

4 cups (946 ml) low-sodium vegetable broth

2 tablespoons (8 g) nutritional yeast (optional)

1 cup (110 g) dry ditalini pasta or similar small pasta shape (gluten-free, if desired)

Yield: 4 to 6 servings

Heat the olive oil in a soup pot over medium heat. Add the onion and sauté for 5 to 6 minutes until soft and translucent. Add the carrots, celery, and bell pepper and sauté 4 to 5 minutes until starting to soften.

Add the parsley, basil, thyme, dill, salt, and flour and stir to combine, scraping up any bits of flour on the bottom of the pot. Slowly pour in ½ cup (120 ml) of milk while whisking continuously, again scraping up any bits of flour on the bottom; a flat whisk is convenient here, but a balloon whisk will work as well. Whisk until the flour is completely incorporated.

Add the remainder of the milk, vegetable broth, and nutritional yeast, if using. Whisk to combine. Increase the heat to high and bring to a boil. Once boiling, add the pasta, and then reduce the heat to medium-low and simmer for 10 to 15 minutes until the pasta is cooked through, stirring often to prevent the pasta from sticking.

Taste and adjust the seasoning, if necessary.

Swap It!

For a gluten-free option, use brown rice flour instead of all-purpose flour.

Tuscan White Bean Soup

This is such a comforting, warming soup. Creamy white beans make this soup hearty and filling, yet light tasting. Superfood kale mingles with familiar vegetables like carrots, celery, and tomatoes. The secret to getting my kids to enjoy the kale is chopping the leaves really small. This allows the kale to soften quickly and makes it easy to eat. Serve this soup with crusty bread.

2 tablespoons (28 ml) olive oil

1 yellow onion, diced

3 cloves garlic, minced

1 cup (130 g) diced carrots
(about 3 medium carrots)

2 ribs celery, diced

2 tablespoons (28 ml) white wine vinegar

1 teaspoon dried thyme

1 teaspoon dried oregano

½ teaspoon dried basil

2 teaspoons salt, or to taste

¼ teaspoon black pepper, or to taste

2 tablespoons (28 ml) tamari,
coconut aminos, or soy sauce
(gluten-free, if desired)

1 can (15 ounces, or 425 g) diced tomatoes

2 cans (15 ounces, or 425 g each)
cannellini beans (white kidney beans),
drained and rinsed

6 cups (1.4 L) low-sodium vegetable broth

3–4 kale leaves, stems removed,
chopped small

¼ cup (15 g) loosely packed fresh
parsley, chopped

Yield: 4 to 6 servings

Heat the olive oil in a large soup pot over medium heat. Add the onion and sauté for 5 to 6 minutes until soft and translucent. Add the garlic, carrots, celery, and white wine vinegar. Sauté for 3 to 4 minutes until the vegetables are starting to soften and the vinegar is mostly absorbed.

Add the thyme, oregano, basil, salt, pepper, tamari, tomatoes, cannellini beans, and vegetable broth. Increase the heat to high and bring to a boil and then reduce the heat to low and simmer for 15 to 20 minutes.

Add the kale and parsley. Stir to combine and heat through.

SERVING SUGGESTION: Serve with a big hunk of crusty bread.

Kids in the Kitchen

Have your kids tear the kale leaves from the woody, fibrous stems before you chop them. They can also drain and rinse the beans in a strainer.

Creamy Potato Soup with Kale and Corn

This is one of the most beloved recipes from my blog. Everyone loves it from adults to teens to kids. It's thick, creamy, and hearty, and it's loaded with healthy vegetables. The secret to this great potato soup is celery salt! It reminds me so much of my childhood and the soup my mom used to make. You'll love it, too!

2 tablespoons (28 ml) olive oil

½ onion, diced

2 cloves garlic, minced

1 carrot, peeled and diced

2 ribs celery, diced

3 cups (700 ml) low-sodium vegetable broth

4 cups (440 g) diced potatoes, peeled (about 5 to 6 medium-size)

½ teaspoon dried dill

½ teaspoon celery salt

½ teaspoon salt, or to taste

¼ teaspoon black pepper, or to taste

½ cup (77 g) fresh or (82 g) frozen corn kernels

1 cup (67 g) chopped kale, woody stems removed (optional)

¼ cup (60 ml) lite coconut milk (optional)

Sriracha or hot pepper sauce

Yield: 4 servings

Heat the olive oil in a soup pot over medium heat. Sauté the onion and garlic for 4 to 5 minutes until they begin to soften. Add the carrot and celery and sauté for 3 to 4 more minutes. Add the vegetable broth, potatoes, dill, celery salt, salt, and pepper. Increase the heat to bring to a boil, reduce the heat to low, and simmer for 15 minutes until the potatoes are tender.

Using an immersion blender, purée about one-quarter to one-third of the soup to create a thick creamy base. Alternatively, take about 2 cups (475 ml) of the soup and carefully purée it in a blender and then return it back to the soup pot.

Add the corn and kale, if using, stir to combine, and simmer for 5 more minutes to heat through. Take off the heat and add the coconut milk, if using.

Serve with a few dashes of sriracha or hot pepper sauce, if desired.

Kids in the Kitchen

Kids can help peel the carrots and help tear the kale leaves from the woody stems. Older kids can help peel the potatoes; I find potatoes a bit harder to peel as they are slippery and oddly shaped.

Lentil Vegetable Soup

This soup is kind of like a protein-packed, hearty minestrone. Use spinach or Swiss chard in place of the kale, if you wish. A squeeze of fresh lemon just before serving brightens everything up.

2 tablespoons (28 ml) olive oil

1 yellow onion, diced

3 cloves garlic, minced

3 carrots, sliced into thin coins (Fatter carrots can be cut in half and then sliced.)

1 zucchini, chopped

1 can (28 ounces, or 785 g) diced tomatoes

1 tablespoon (6 g) Italian seasoning

½ teaspoon paprika

½ teaspoon black pepper, or to taste

1½ cups (288 g) dry brown or green lentils, picked over and rinsed well with cold water

4 cups (946 ml) low-sodium vegetable broth, plus more if you like a thinner soup

1 teaspoon salt, or to taste

2–3 kale leaves, chopped small, woody stems removed

1 fresh lemon

Yield: 4 to 6 servings

Heat the olive oil in a large soup pot over medium heat. Add the onion and sauté for 5 to 6 minutes until soft and translucent. Add the garlic and carrots and sauté for 1 to 2 minutes. Add the zucchini, tomatoes, Italian seasoning, paprika, and pepper and stir to combine.

Add the lentils and vegetable broth, increase the heat to high to bring to a boil, and then decrease the heat to medium-low. Simmer for 30 to 35 minutes until the lentils are tender. If you like a thinner soup, feel free to add more broth to your liking.

Add the salt, kale, and a squeeze of fresh lemon. Taste and adjust the seasoning, if necessary.

NOTE: Salt and acidic ingredients could hinder the lentils from cooking properly and becoming tender, so be sure to wait until after they are cooked through before adding the salt and lemon juice.

Mixed Lentil Quinoa Soup

This soup reminds me of my favorite ready-to-eat soup from Trader Joe's: Lentil Soup with Ancient Grains. The TJ's soup uses quinoa, amaranth, and millet, but we're using only quinoa here for convenience. Two kinds of lentils are the secret to the substance of this soup. The red lentils cook quickly and nearly disappear into the soup, giving it body, while the green lentils retain their shape and offer texture.

2 tablespoons (28 ml) olive oil

1 yellow onion, diced

2 cloves garlic, minced

2 ribs celery, diced

2 carrots, peeled and diced

1 cup (192 g) dry red lentils, picked over and rinsed well with cold water

1 cup (192 g) dry brown or green lentils, picked over and rinsed well with cold water

½ cup (87 g) dry quinoa, rinsed well with cold water

1 can (28 ounces, or 785 g) diced tomatoes

6 cups (1.4 L) low-sodium vegetable broth

2 tablespoons (28 ml) tamari, coconut aminos, or soy sauce (gluten-free, if desired)

1 tablespoon (7 g) cumin

1 tablespoon (7 g) smoked paprika

1 teaspoon dried thyme

1 teaspoon dried oregano

1 teaspoon salt, or to taste

½ teaspoon dried basil

½ teaspoon ground nutmeg

Handful of fresh parsley, chopped (about ¼ cup [15 g] loosely packed, before chopping)

Yield: 6 servings

Heat the olive oil in a large soup pot over medium heat. Add the onion and sauté for 4 to 5 minutes until softened and translucent. Add the garlic, celery, and carrots and sauté for 3 to 4 minutes until starting to soften.

Add the remaining ingredients, except the fresh parsley. Increase the heat to high to bring to a boil and then reduce the heat to medium-low. Simmer for 35 to 40 minutes until the lentils are tender, stirring occasionally to prevent sticking. The red lentils should be unrecognizable as they will break down and become part of the soup base.

Add the chopped parsley and stir through just before serving.

Kids in the Kitchen

Have your kids rinse the lentils and quinoa in mesh strainer over the sink. They can portion out spices, add ingredients to the pot, and help stir.

Rustic Winter Stew

This soup is the one you'll want to go to when it's cold outside. It warms you from the inside out and brings so much comforting flavor. The squash and carrots bring a slight sweetness that the kids really enjoy.

2 tablespoons (28 ml) olive oil

1 yellow onion, diced

2 cloves garlic, minced

3 cups (330 g) peeled and diced yellow or red potato

2 cups (280 g) peeled and diced butternut squash

1 cup (130 g) peeled and diced carrots

1 cup (110 g) peeled and diced parsnips

4 cups (946 ml) low-sodium vegetable broth

2 teaspoons dried thyme

1 teaspoon dried rosemary

½ teaspoon salt, or to taste

¼ teaspoon black pepper, or to taste

2 tablespoons (28 ml) tamari, coconut aminos, or soy sauce (gluten-free, if desired; optional)

Yield: 4 servings

Heat the olive oil in a soup pot over medium heat. Sauté the onion for 5 to 6 minutes until softened and translucent. Add the garlic and sauté for 1 minute. Add the potato, squash, carrots, parsnips, vegetable broth, thyme, rosemary, salt, and pepper. Stir, increase the heat to bring to a boil, and then reduce the heat to low and simmer for 20 minutes or until the vegetables are tender.

Taste and add the tamari for more depth of flavor, if needed.

Remove from the heat. Using a potato masher, mash the vegetables so they break a part a bit, but are still chunky. We like it rustic like this, but if you prefer a smoother soup, you could use an immersion blender and purée to your desired consistency. Alternatively, you don't have to mash or purée any of the soup. It's great as is!

Kids in the Kitchen

Once the soup has cooled slightly, have your kids help mash the vegetables.

CHAPTER 3

Satisfying Salads

Salads don't have to be boring plates of lettuce. They are a great way to offer a variety of healthy vegetables, but they can also include fruits, pasta, beans, grains, nuts, and seeds. Smaller serving sizes of the salads in this chapter can be sides or starters, but don't be afraid to fill a big bowl and eat a salad as a meal.

Very Berry Quinoa Salad
with Cinnamon Toasted Pecans

This salad is light and fresh yet has plenty of protein from the quinoa and pecans. Fresh summer berries are little powerhouses of vitamins and are super kid-friendly. The toasted pecans take this dish to the next level.

FOR THE QUINOA:

1 cup (173 g) tri-color dry quinoa, rinsed well with cold water (or any color quinoa)

1¼ cups (295 ml) water

FOR THE CINNAMON TOASTED PECANS:

1½ tablespoons (30 g) pure maple syrup

1 tablespoon (9 g) coconut sugar or (15 g) brown sugar

½ teaspoon ground cinnamon

Pinch of salt

1 cup (110 g) pecan halves

1 teaspoon coconut oil

FOR THE SALAD:

6 cups (330 g) mixed baby salad greens

2 cups (weight will vary) fresh mixed berries (blueberries, blackberries, raspberries, strawberries, etc.)

1 recipe Maple Dijon Vinaigrette (page 163)

Yield: 4 servings

For the Quinoa: Combine the quinoa and water in a small pot and bring to a boil. Cover, reduce the heat to medium-low, and simmer for 12 to 15 minutes until the quinoa is tender and the liquid is absorbed. Fluff with a fork.

For the Cinnamon Toasted Pecans: Line a large plate with parchment paper and set aside. In a small bowl, whisk together the maple syrup, sugar, cinnamon, and salt. Add the pecans and stir to coat evenly.

Heat the coconut oil in a nonstick skillet over medium heat. Pour the pecans in the skillet, spreading them out in an even layer. Cook for 4 to 5 minutes, stirring frequently, until toasted. Nuts can burn quickly, so don't walk away at this point! You'll know the pecans are done when you start to smell them. Pour them out onto the parchment-lined plate and spread in an even layer. Let them cool. They will crisp up as they cool.

For the Salad: Combine the mixed baby greens, mixed berries, cooked quinoa, and toasted pecans in a large salad bowl. Mix well. To serve, divide among 4 bowls and drizzle with the Maple Dijon Vinaigrette.

Swap It!

Try using romaine, red leaf lettuce, or arugula instead of the mixed baby greens to change it up.

Kids in the Kitchen

Have your kids add all the ingredients to a big salad bowl and get their clean hands in there and mix it all up!

Black Bean Citrus Quinoa Salad

This salad is light and bright with fresh veggies and citrus, yet the quinoa and black beans make it incredibly filling. I love taking this dish to potlucks and watching it disappear!

1 cup (173 g) dry quinoa, rinsed well with cold water

1¼ cups (295 ml) water

¼ cup (60 ml) extra-virgin olive oil

¼ cup (60 ml) fresh lime juice

1 tablespoon (15 ml) apple cider vinegar

¼ teaspoon salt, or to taste

⅛ teaspoon black pepper, or to taste

1 can (15 ounces, or 425 g) black beans, drained and rinsed

1 English cucumber, diced

1 pint (275 g) grape tomatoes, halved

¼ cup (40 g) diced red onion

4 mandarin oranges (such as clementines), peeled and segmented

Yield: 4 to 6 servings

Add the quinoa and water to a pot on the stove and bring to a boil. Cover, reduce the heat to medium-low, and simmer for 12 to 15 minutes until the water is absorbed and the quinoa is tender. Fluff with a fork.

Meanwhile, whisk together the extra-virgin olive oil, lime juice, apple cider vinegar, salt, and pepper. Set aside.

Add the cooked quinoa to a large mixing bowl and add the black beans, cucumber, tomatoes, onion, and mandarin oranges. Pour in the dressing and mix well to combine.

This salad can be eaten immediately, at room temperature, or cold.

Add It!

I sometimes chop up a head of romaine lettuce and toss it with the rest of the ingredients, making it stretch even further.

Lentil Salad with Cauliflower and Grapes

Cauliflower tossed with turmeric and curry powder, roasted until tender and golden, and then tossed with protein-packed lentils and sweet, juicy grapes—it's flavor and texture dynamite! This salad is delicious served warm or at room temperature. It's perfect for lunch on-the-go!

FOR THE ROASTED CAULIFLOWER SALAD:

1 head cauliflower, chopped into florets

½ red onion, sliced thin

1 tablespoon (15 ml) olive oil

1 teaspoon ground turmeric

½ teaspoon yellow curry powder

¼ teaspoon salt, or to taste

1 cup (180 g) halved red seedless grapes

½ cup (96 g) dry brown or green lentils, picked over and rinsed well in cold water

1½ cups (355 ml) water or vegetable broth

FOR THE DRESSING
(MAKES ABOUT ½ CUP [120 ML]):

2 tablespoons (32 g) raw creamy almond butter

3 tablespoons (45 ml) fresh lemon juice

2 tablespoons (40 g) pure maple syrup

¾ teaspoon ground turmeric

¼ teaspoon yellow curry powder

2–3 tablespoons (28–45 ml) water, to thin

¼ teaspoon salt, or to taste

Yield: 4 servings

For the Roasted Cauliflower Salad: Preheat the oven to 400°F (200°C, or gas mark 6). Line a rimmed baking sheet with parchment paper and set aside.

In a large bowl, toss the cauliflower florets and onion with olive oil, turmeric, curry powder, and salt. Spread in an even layer on the prepared baking sheet. Bake for 25 minutes until the cauliflower is tender and the onion starts to caramelize.

In the meantime, bring the lentils and water to a boil, cover, and turn the heat down to medium-low. Simmer for 15 to 20 minutes until tender, but not mushy.

When everything is cooked through, in a large bowl, toss the cauliflower-and-onion mixture with the lentils and add in the red grapes.

For the Dressing: Whisk all the dressing ingredients together in a small bowl, adding just enough water until you reach your desired consistency.

Drizzle some of the dressing lightly over the salad and serve with extra dressing on the side.

Kids in the Kitchen

Have the kids break the cauliflower into florets, halve the grapes, and whisk the dressing.

Mediterranean Pasta Salad

Perfect for those summer days that call for lightened up dishes, yet it still feels like a comfort food dish, just as pasta should. All you need are a few pantry staples and about twenty minutes. It's perfect for a busy weeknight meal.

16 ounces (455 g) penne pasta or pasta of choice (gluten-free, if desired)

2 tablespoons (28 ml) olive oil

2 cloves garlic, minced

1 jar (12 ounces, or 340 g) roasted red peppers, drained and chopped

1 jar (12 ounces, or 340 g) artichoke hearts, drained and chopped

1 pint (275 g) cherry tomatoes, halved

Juice and zest of 1 lemon, plus more if needed

1 tablespoon (3 g) dried oregano

Salt and black pepper

¼ cup (25 g) sliced pitted Greek olives (optional)

Yield: 4 servings

Cook the penne according to package directions.

Meanwhile, heat the olive oil in a large skillet over medium heat. Add the garlic and cook for 1 minute until fragrant.

Add the roasted red peppers, artichoke hearts, and tomatoes. Cook, stirring frequently, until the veggies start to give off some liquid, about 15 minutes.

Add the lemon juice, lemon zest, oregano, salt, pepper, and olives, if using. Stir and cook for 1 to 2 minutes to combine the flavors.

Once the pasta is cooked, drain and add to the vegetables. Toss well to combine. Taste and adjust the seasoning, if necessary. Add another squeeze of lemon, an extra dash of salt, or perhaps some Greek olives and a drizzle of olive oil, if desired.

Serve right away or store it in the fridge until ready to eat. This dish is delicious warm, room temperature, or cold!

Kids in the Kitchen

Have the kids halve the tomatoes and zest the lemon.

Black Bean and Rice Kale Salad

This salad is inspired by one I had at Tropical Smoothie Café called the Hummus Veggie Bowl. Their version contains cheese and ranch dressing, which I always ask to leave out, and instead make my own "dressing" out of the salad ingredients. I mash the diced avocado and hummus into the salad and stir it well, and just like that, my salad is coated in a dressing. In this version, I'm making an actual avocado dressing to massage into the kale and topping off the whole thing with a generous dollop of hummus. Avocado and hummus might seem like a strange combo at first, but trust me, it's so good!

1 avocado, peel and pit removed, halves divided

Juice of ½ lemon, plus more to taste

½ teaspoon salt, or to taste

¼ teaspoon black pepper, or to taste

¼ teaspoon ground turmeric

⅓ cup (80 ml) extra-virgin olive oil

1 bunch kale, woody stems removed, chopped into small bite-size pieces

1 cup (195 g) cooked brown rice

1 can (15 ounces, or 425 g) black beans, drained and rinsed

2 tomatoes, diced

½ cup (160 g) Quick Pickled Red Onions (page 170)

1½ cups (370 g) Hummus (recipe below or store-bought)

FOR THE HUMMUS:

1 can (15 ounces, or 425 g) chickpeas, drained and rinsed

1 clove garlic

2 tablespoons (30 g) tahini

½ teaspoon cumin

2 tablespoons (28 ml) fresh lemon juice

½ teaspoon salt, or to taste

2 tablespoons (28 ml) extra-virgin olive oil

Water to thin as needed

Yield: 4 to 6 servings

Whisk or blend together one half of the avocado, lemon juice, ½ teaspoon of salt, pepper, turmeric, and extra-virgin olive oil. Pour over the kale in a large bowl. Mix it around well so the dressing covers all the kale. Now, with clean hands, get in there and massage the dressing into the kale by rubbing the leaves for about 2 minutes. This will soften the kale to make it easier to chew and make it more flavorful.

Dice the remaining half of the avocado and add it to the kale along with the cooked brown rice, black beans, tomatoes, and Quick Pickled Red Onions and toss to combine.

For the Hummus: In a food processor, combine all the ingredients, except the water, and purée until smooth. Add water, 1 tablespoon (15 ml) at a time until the desired consistency is reached.

Portion the salad out in individual bowls and top each one with a generous dollop of Hummus.

Swap It!

Any gains would work in this salad in place of the rice—quinoa, couscous, millet, or farro. Use whatever you have leftover in your fridge.

Black Bean Taco Salad
with Crunchy Roasted Chickpeas

This is another recipe from my blog that always gets rave reviews! It has all the flavors and textures of traditional taco salad with a vegetarian twist. The crunchy chickpeas are a healthy stand-in for greasy fried tortilla strips. And the Creamy Cumin Ranch Dressing knocks it out of the park!

FOR THE CRUNCHY ROASTED CHICKPEAS:

1 can (15 ounces, or 425 g) chickpeas, rinsed, drained and dried well

1 teaspoon chili powder

1 teaspoon cumin

½ teaspoon salt

¼ teaspoon ground cinnamon

FOR THE BLACK BEANS:

1 can (15 ounces, or 425 g) black beans, rinsed and drained

2 teaspoons chili powder

½ teaspoon salt, or to taste

½ teaspoon garlic powder

½ teaspoon smoked paprika

1 teaspoon cumin

½ teaspoon cayenne (optional)

¼ cup (60 ml) water

FOR THE SALAD:

1 head green leaf or romaine lettuce, chopped

1–2 tomatoes, diced

1 red bell pepper, seeded and diced

1 avocado, peeled and pit removed, diced

1 cup (164 g) fresh or thawed corn kernels

FOR THE DRESSING:

1 recipe Creamy Cumin Ranch Dressing (page 162)

Yield: 4 servings

Preheat the oven to 400°F (200°C, or gas mark 6). Line a rimmed baking sheet with parchment paper and set aside.

For the Crunchy Roasted Chickpeas: Toss the chickpeas with the chili powder, cumin, salt, and cinnamon. Place the chickpeas on the prepared baking sheet in one even layer. Bake for 20 to 30 minutes, shaking the pan every 10 minutes. The chickpeas should be slightly crunchy; they will continue to crisp up as they cool. Set aside.

For the Black Beans: Toss the black beans with all the spices and warm in a pan over medium heat with ¼ cup (60 ml) of water. Stir occasionally until warmed through, about 5 to 6 minutes.

For the Salad: To assemble the salad, toss the lettuce, tomatoes, bell pepper, avocado, and corn in a large bowl. Plate the salad mixture on each plate or bowl. Divide the black beans among the plates and top with Crunchy Roasted Chickpeas. Drizzle with Creamy Cumin Ranch Dressing.

NOTE: The spice mixture isn't spicy hot, so it's great for kids, too. If you'd like added heat, try adding ½ teaspoon chipotle powder to the black beans or topping your salad with a drizzle of spicy salsa.

Kids in the Kitchen

The kids can toss the chickpeas with the spices and pour them onto the baking sheet. They can also stir the spices into the black beans. And hand over the salad spinner and let them spin the rinsed lettuce.

BBQ Ranch Romaine Pasta Salad

This salad has it all—crunchy veggies, protein-packed beans, creamy avocado, and kid-friendly noodles. Plus, it has a sweet tangy BBQ dressing that's easily made in a blender. This is one salad even your kids will crave!

FOR THE SALAD:

1 cup (112 g) ditalini pasta

2 heads romaine lettuce, chopped (about 6 cups [282 g])

1 can (15 ounces, or 425 g) black beans, drained and rinsed (or 1½ cups [258 g] cooked beans)

1 cup (164 g) fresh or thawed corn kernels

1 cup (110 g) shredded carrots

2 tomatoes, diced

1 avocado, peel and pit removed, diced

¼ cup (4 g) chopped cilantro

FOR THE BBQ RANCH DRESSING (MAKES ABOUT 1 CUP [235 ml]):

½ cup (70 g) raw cashews (soaked in warm water for at least 20 minutes if you don't have a high-speed blender)

½ cup (120 ml) water, plus more if needed

½ teaspoon salt, or to taste

½ teaspoon onion powder

½ teaspoon dried parsley

¼ teaspoon dried dill

¼ teaspoon garlic powder

2 tablespoons (28 ml) fresh lemon juice

¼ cup (60 ml) Sweet-and-Spicy BBQ Sauce (page 165) or store-bought BBQ sauce

Yield: 4 servings

Cook the pasta according to package directions. Drain and add to a large salad bowl.

To the bowl, add the romaine, black beans, corn, carrots, tomatoes, avocado, and cilantro.

For the BBQ Ranch Dressing: Purée all the ingredients in a blender. Add additional water 1 tablespoon (15 ml) at a time, if needed to thin.

Drizzle the BBQ Ranch Dressing over the salad in individual bowls.

Kids in the Kitchen

Have your kids purée the dressing in the blender. Double check they have the lid on tight!

Cherry Almond Couscous Salad
with Butternut Squash and Apples

This recipe is inspired by a Stuffed Acorn Squash recipe in the cookbook *Vegan Yum Yum* by Lauren Ulm. Instead of using the couscous as a stuffing, the squash is diced along with some apples for a sweet and tart contrast and then mixed with the couscous all together in one bowl over healthy greens.

2½ cups (350 g) diced butternut squash (about 1-inch [2.5 cm] size cubes)

2 teaspoons olive oil

¾ teaspoon salt, or to taste, divided

¼ teaspoon black pepper, or to taste

½ teaspoon ground cinnamon

½ cup (80 g) dried cherries

½ cup (73 g) raw almonds

1½ cups (355 ml) water

1 cup (175 g) dry couscous

4 cups (120 g) baby spinach or greens of choice

1 tart apple, chopped

2 scallions, sliced

1 recipe Maple Dijon Vinaigrette (page 163)

Yield: 4 servings

Preheat the oven to 400°F (200°C, or gas mark 6). Line a rimmed baking sheet with parchment paper and set aside.

Toss the butternut squash with olive oil, ¼ teaspoon of salt, pepper, and cinnamon. Mix well to coat evenly. Spread onto the prepared baking sheet in one even layer. Roast for 15 minutes, gently stir the squash and spread back out in an even layer, and roast for 10 more minutes until tender.

Meanwhile, place the dried cherries, almonds, and water in a pot on the stove. Bring to a boil, add the couscous, cover, and remove from the heat. Let sit for 5 minutes and then fluff with a fork.

Toss the spinach, apple, and scallions in a salad bowl. Top with the couscous mixture and roasted butternut squash. Drizzle with the Maple Dijon Vinaigrette (you may not use it all) and toss to coat evenly.

TIP: Prechopped butternut squash is fairly easy to find in grocery stores these days. It's a great time-saver!

NOTE: We like big chunks of whole almonds, but if you prefer, feel free to chop them smaller.

Very Veggie Quinoa Salad

This is a great option for a quick summer dinner. Quinoa cooks in just fifteen minutes and the rest of the ingredients are served raw, so it's very fast and easy. Although this salad is hearty enough on its own, it also makes a great side dish. It's one of my go-to potluck dishes because it can sit out for a while and won't go bad. I've also been known to pack it up in a container and take it for lunch or dinner on-the-go during those crazy days when we have a never-ending schedule of kids' activities. Don't forget to pack the forks!

1¼ cups (285 ml) water

¾ cups (128 g) dry quinoa, rinsed well with cold water

1 small head broccoli, chopped small (about 2 cups [142 g])

2 sweet bell peppers, seeded and diced (see note)

1 English cucumber, chopped (about 2 cups [270 g])

1 cup (150 g) halved seedless red grapes

¼ cup (15 g) chopped fresh parsley

2 tablespoons (8 g) chopped fresh dill

¼ cup (36 g) raw shelled sunflower seeds

2 tablespoons (18 g) hulled hemp seeds

1 recipe Maple Dijon Vinaigrette (page 163)

Yield: 4 servings

In a small saucepot, bring the water to a boil. Once boiling, add the quinoa. Cover the pot, reduce the heat to medium-low, and simmer for 12 to 15 minutes until the liquid is absorbed and the quinoa is tender. Fluff with a fork. Let cool.

Meanwhile, add the remaining ingredients to a large bowl. Mix well. When the quinoa is done and cooled, add it to the vegetable mixture. Mix well.

Serve immediately or store in an airtight container in the fridge until ready to serve. This salad should keep for 2 to 3 days.

NOTE: We like using an orange and yellow bell pepper for this salad. Red bell peppers are also a good choice. I find green bell peppers to be a bit too strong for this dish.

SERVING SUGGESTION: This salad can be served cold or room temperature. Add in some chopped leafy greens for added bulk if you wish.

Kids in the Kitchen

Kids can rinse the quinoa in a small mesh strainer. Depending on their skill level, they can help you chop the vegetables. Kids of all ages can help whisk the dressing and mix the salad when ready.

CHAPTER 4

Loaded Handhelds

Sandwiches aren't just for lunch boxes! The ingredient possibilities are endless—just about anything can be packed between two slices of bread, stuffed into a pita or wrap, folded up in a tortilla, or laid out open-face as a pizza or baguette. Many of these are indeed suitable for a lunch box, but all of them make yummy dinners. And who doesn't love to eat with their hands? I find that the messier the meal, the more my kids love it!

Spicy Hummus Veggie Wraps

It doesn't get much easier than using store-bought coleslaw or broccoli slaw mix. I love the contrast of the spicy hummus, the sweet apple, and the tangy slaw. This wrap also has texture contrast between the hummus, slaw, apple, and tortilla. Veggie sandwiches do not have to be boring!

FOR THE SPICY HUMMUS:

1 can (15 ounces, or 425 g) chickpeas, drained and rinsed (or 1½ cups [246 g] cooked chickpeas)

1 clove garlic

2 tablespoons (30 g) tahini

½ teaspoon cumin

2 tablespoons (28 ml) fresh lemon juice

¼ teaspoon salt, or to taste

¼ cup (65 g) spicy salsa

FOR THE VEGGIE WRAPS:

2 cups (200 g) coleslaw mix or broccoli slaw mix

¼ cup (60 g) plant-based plain yogurt

1 tablespoon (15 ml) fresh lemon juice

Dash of salt and black pepper, or to taste

4 large tortillas (gluten-free, if desired)

1 cup (246 g) Spicy Hummus or store-bought

2 big handfuls of baby spinach or leafy green of choice

1 crisp apple, sliced thin

Yield: 4 servings

For the Spicy Hummus: Place all the ingredients in the bowl of a food processor. Process until smooth, stopping the machine and scraping down the sides occasionally, if needed.

For the Veggie Wraps: Mix the coleslaw mix, yogurt, lemon juice, salt, and pepper in a mixing bowl. Set aside.

Lay out one tortilla on a clean flat surface. Spread about ¼ cup (62 g) of Spicy Hummus all over the surface of the tortilla. Place some spinach leaves on top of the Spicy Hummus. On half of the tortilla, pile ½ cup (50 g) of the coleslaw mix and one-quarter of the apple slices.

Fold in the sides of the tortilla and then, starting with the end that has the slaw and apples, roll tightly. Cut in half. Repeat with the remaining tortillas and ingredients.

TIP: The Spicy Hummus can be made ahead of time and kept covered in the fridge for several days. Don't be afraid to use a spicy salsa for this recipe as the other ingredients will help to mellow out the heat.

Add It!

Feel free to add a sprinkle of sunflower seeds or crushed walnuts for extra protein and crunch.

Kids in the Kitchen

Have your kids make the hummus under your supervision. They can also mix the coleslaw with the yogurt and lemon juice. They can even add all the ingredients to their own wraps!

Curried Tofu Salad Sandwiches

Crumbled firm tofu, crisp celery, and juicy apples mingle among a creamy, tangy curry dressing. It's perfect on its own, with crackers, or piled high on a sandwich. Quick and easy to make—and it's even better the next day.

½ cup (85 g) unsweetened plant-based plain yogurt

2 tablespoons (28 g) plant-based mayo

1 tablespoon (15 g) Dijon mustard

1 tablespoon (15 ml) fresh lemon juice

2½ teaspoons (5 g) yellow curry powder

½ teaspoon ground turmeric

½ teaspoon salt, or to taste

⅛ teaspoon black pepper, or to taste

1 package (14 ounces, or 390 g) firm or extra-firm tofu, drained and pressed (see note)

1 rib celery, diced

1 sweet apple, cored and diced

2 scallions, diced

1 tablespoon (4 g) chopped fresh parsley

12 slices bread (gluten-free, if desired)

Lettuce and tomato slices, for serving (optional)

Yield: 6 sandwiches

In a medium mixing bowl, whisk the yogurt, mayo, Dijon mustard, lemon juice, curry powder, turmeric, salt, and pepper.

With your clean hands, crumble the tofu in the same bowl. Don't be perfect; leave some pieces bigger than others and crumble some pieces smaller. This will help give the salad extra texture.

Add the celery, apple, scallions, and parsley to the tofu. Mix well until everything is well covered in the creamy curry dressing.

You can enjoy this right away or store it in the fridge to let the flavors come together even more.

When ready to eat, toast the bread, if desired. Pile about ½ cup (130 g) of the curried tofu onto one slice of bread. Add lettuce and tomato, if desired. Top with another slice of bread.

TIP: To press the tofu, wrap the block of tofu in several paper towels or a clean kitchen towel and place on a plate. Place another plate on top of the tofu and weigh down the top plate. Cans or bags of beans or rice work well for this or a heavy skillet. This tower may start to topple as the tofu loses liquid, so don't use anything breakable, like glass jars, as a weight. Press for about 20 minutes.

Swap It!

To make this soy-free, use 2 cans (15 ounces, or 425 g each) of chickpeas, drained and rinsed, instead of tofu. Smash them with a potato masher or fork.

Chickpea Salad Sandwiches

This recipe is a great example of how easy it is to transition to a plant-based diet. I used to make this recipe using chicken many, many years ago. It was my go-to potluck dish and everyone loved it. When I changed my diet, I didn't want to give up this deliciousness, so I swapped out the chicken for chickpeas. It's still one of my go-to potluck dishes and everyone from herbivores to omnivores loves it! It's quick and easy and makes the perfect lunch or dinner. Load it up between two slices of bread, on a cracker, or over lettuce as a salad.

2 cans (15 ounces, or 425 g each) chickpeas, drained and rinsed

2 ribs celery, diced

3 scallions, sliced

1 cup (150 g) red seedless grapes, halved

¼ cup (60 g) plant-based mayo

1 tablespoon (15 g) Dijon mustard

1 teaspoon dried dill

1 teaspoon poultry seasoning

½ teaspoon salt, or to taste

¼ teaspoon black pepper, or to taste

12 slices bread (gluten-free, if desired)

Lettuce, for serving (optional)

Yield: 6 sandwiches

In a medium bowl, mash the chickpeas with a potato masher or fork. Add the remaining ingredients and mix well.

Toast the bread, if desired. Pile the Chickpea Salad onto one slice of bread. Add lettuce, if desired. Top with another slice of bread. Repeat with the remaining ingredients.

Kids in the Kitchen

Hand over the potato masher and let your kids do the manual labor! They can also halve the grapes, portion out the spices, and mix it all together.

Thai Chickpea Tortilla Wraps

Kids love anything with peanut butter, so this wrap with a peanut butter–based sauce is a great way to get them to eat their veggies.

2 cans (15 ounces, or 425 g each) chickpeas, drained and rinsed, divided (or 3 cups [492 g] cooked chickpeas)

2 cups (200 g) coleslaw mix

2 scallions, chopped

½ English cucumber, diced

Handful of fresh cilantro, chopped

¼ cup (35 g) chopped peanuts (raw or roasted unsalted)

¼ cup (65 g) smooth peanut butter

3 tablespoons (45 ml) tamari, coconut aminos, or soy sauce (gluten-free, if desired)

2 tablespoons (28 ml) fresh lime juice

2 tablespoons (40 g) pure maple syrup

2 tablespoons (28 ml) toasted sesame oil

Sriracha (optional)

4 tortillas (10 inches, or 25 cm each) (gluten-free, if desired)

4 large lettuce leaves

Yield: 4 servings

In a large mixing bowl, add 1 can of chickpeas and smash them using a potato masher or large fork. Add the other can of chickpeas, coleslaw mix, scallions, cucumber, cilantro, and chopped peanuts. Mix well.

In a small bowl, whisk the peanut butter, tamari, lime juice, maple syrup, toasted sesame oil, and a dash of sriracha, if using. Pour onto the chickpea mixture and stir well to combine.

Lay down one tortilla and place one large lettuce leaf on top. Place 1 cup (250 g) of the chickpea mixture on one end of the tortilla and roll it up tightly, tucking in the sides and you go. Slice it in half. Repeat with the remaining tortillas and chickpea mixture. Serve immediately.

Swap It!

Serve the chickpea mixture in the lettuce leaves and skip the tortillas for a lower-carb option.

Kids in the Kitchen

This is such an easy recipe; the kids can probably make it all on their own. Stand by for supervision and to help with chopping, if needed.

Falafel Pitas with Quick Pickled Red Onions and Lemon-Dill-Tahini Sauce

These easy falafel pitas are loaded with flavor and texture. They're fresh, creamy, crunchy, and savory. My kids like to dip the falafel patties into the Lemon-Dill-Tahini Sauce and eat the cucumbers and tomatoes on the side. I often send these pitas in their lunch boxes.

FOR THE FALAFEL:

3 tablespoons (45 ml) olive oil, divided

½ red onion, diced

3 cloves garlic, minced

1 can (15 ounces, or 425 g) chickpeas, drained and rinsed (or 1½ cups [246 g] cooked chickpeas)

¼ cup (15 g) fresh parsley

¼ cup (4 g) fresh cilantro

2 tablespoons (16 g) sesame seeds

1 teaspoon cumin

1 teaspoon coriander

½ teaspoon turmeric

½ teaspoon paprika

½ teaspoon salt, or to taste

⅓ cup (30 g) chickpea flour (All-purpose flour or a gluten-free flour blend will work as well.)

FOR THE LEMON-DILL-TAHINI SAUCE:

½ cup (115 g) plain plant-based yogurt

2 tablespoons (30 g) tahini

Juice of ½ lemon

½ teaspoon garlic powder, or to taste

¼ teaspoon salt, or to taste

1 tablespoon (4 g) chopped fresh dill

For the Falafel: Heat 1 tablespoon (15 ml) of olive oil in a small skillet over medium heat. Add the onion and garlic and sauté for 4 to 5 minutes until soft.

In the bowl of a food processor, add the sautéed onions and garlic along with all the remaining falafel ingredients, except the remaining olive oil. Pulse until well combined, but NOT puréed. The mixture should be it a bit chunky. It may look loose and crumbly but should hold together well when pressed in your hand.

Form 2 tablespoons (28 g) of the falafel mixture into a ball with your hands and flatten into a patty. Set aside. Repeat with the remaining falafel mixture. You should have 11 to 12 falafel patties.

Wipe out the skillet you used for the onions and garlic and heat another tablespoon (15 ml) of of oil over medium heat. Add half of the falafel patties and cook for 3 to 4 minutes until golden brown on the bottom. Gently flip them over and cook for another 3 to 4 minutes until golden brown on the second side. Add the final tablespoon of olive oil (15 ml) and repeat with the remaining falafel patties.

For the Lemon-Dill-Tahini Sauce: Whisk all the ingredients in a small bowl. Taste and adjust the seasoning.

Kids in the Kitchen

Your kids can help you form the falafel mixture into patties. They can also whisk the Lemon-Dill-Tahini Sauce.

FOR THE PITA POCKETS:

4 pita pocket halves

Green leaf lettuce

Sliced tomatoes

Sliced cucumbers

Quick Pickled Red Onions (page 170)

Yield: 4 servings

To assemble the pita pockets: Add a leaf or two of lettuce to one pita pocket, followed by a slice or two of tomato, 2 to 3 slices of cucumber, 2 to 3 falafel patties, and several slices Quick Pickled Red Onions. Drizzle with the Lemon-Dill-Tahini Sauce.

Sloppy BBQ Chickpea Sandwiches

Sweet and mildly spicy, hearty and delicious, this sloppy sandwich is husband, kid, and carnivore approved! The easy coleslaw is the perfect cooling contrast to the BBQ sauce. It comes together quickly and easily. You're going to want seconds!

FOR THE CHEATER VEGAN COLESLAW:

½ cup (85 g) plant-based mayo

2 tablespoons (28 ml) apple cider vinegar

1 tablespoon (20 g) pure maple syrup

1 teaspoon yellow mustard

¼ teaspoon celery salt

1 package (14 ounces, or 390 g) store-bought coleslaw mix

1 tablespoon (1 g) chopped fresh cilantro (optional)

FOR THE PINEAPPLE CHICKPEA BBQ SANDWICHES:

1 recipe Sweet-and-Spicy BBQ Sauce (page 165)

2 cans (15 ounces, or 425 g each) chickpeas, rinsed and drained (or 3 cups [492 g] cooked chickpeas)

¼ red onion, diced

1 can (15 ounces, or 425 g) crushed pineapple, drained

¼ cup (4 g) chopped fresh cilantro

8 burger buns (gluten-free, if desired)

1 recipe Cheater Vegan Coleslaw

Pickle slices (optional)

Yield: 8 servings

For the Cheater Vegan Coleslaw: In a medium mixing bowl, whisk together the mayo, apple cider vinegar, maple syrup, yellow mustard, and celery salt. Add the coleslaw mix and toss well until everything is well covered.

Refrigerate until ready to use. Sprinkle on fresh cilantro, if using, for garnish just before serving.

For the Pineapple Chickpea BBQ Sandwiches: Make the Sweet-and-Spicy BBQ Sauce. While it cooks, add one can of chickpeas to a large mixing bowl. Mash the chickpeas with a potato masher or a fork. Add the other can of chickpeas, onion, pineapple, and cilantro.

When the Sweet-and-Spicy BBQ Sauce is done simmering and has thickened up to your liking, add the chickpea mixture and stir well. Simmer for another 5 to 10 minutes to heat through.

To serve, scoop some of the BBQ chickpeas onto a bun. Top with the Cheater Vegan Coleslaw and sliced pickles, if desired. Devour.

TIP: The Sweet-and-Spicy BBQ Sauce and the Cheater Vegan Coleslaw can be made ahead of time and kept in the fridge. When ready to eat, this meal can be ready in about 15 minutes!

Kids in the Kitchen

Have your kids mix the coleslaw ingredients and mash the chickpeas.

Spicy Chickpea Melts

These melty sandwiches are ridiculously easy. They're reminiscent of a tuna melt but made with healthy plant protein instead. It's worth the splurge for plant-based store-bought cheese for these!

1 can (15 ounces, or 425 g) chickpeas, drained and rinsed (or 1½ cups [246 g] cooked chickpeas)

3 tablespoons (48 g) spicy tomato-based salsa

2 tablespoons (28 g) plant-based mayo

1 rib celery, diced

2 tablespoons (18 g) chopped dill pickles (We like the spicy pickles!)

2 teaspoons Old Bay seasoning (see note)

4 slices bread or baguette (gluten-free, if desired)

2–3 tablespoons (28–42 g) plant-based butter

4 slices plant-based Mozzarella or Provolone cheese

Yield: 4 servings

Preheat the oven to 350°F (180°C, or gas mark 4).

With a potato masher or a fork, mash the chickpeas in a bowl with the salsa and mayo. Add the celery, chopped pickles, and Old Bay. Mix well.

Place 4 slices of bread or baguette on a baking sheet. Spread butter on each slice of bread. Top each slice of bread with 3 to 4 tablespoons (45 to 62 g) of chickpea mixture. Top with a slice of cheese.

Bake for 10 minutes. Turn the oven to broil and place them under the broiler for another 1 minute until the cheese is bubbly. Remove from the oven and let cool for a few minutes.

Cut the Chickpea Melts in half, if desired, and serve.

TIP: Double it! For big appetites or to feed a crowd, this recipe will easily double to serve 2 sandwiches per person.

NOTE: I don't often buy store-bought vegan cheese, opting instead to make my own cheesy sauces, but sometimes you just can't beat the convenience of ready-made. There are many good brands out there these days. Field Roast Chao, Follow Your Heart Smoked Gouda, and Daiya Cutting Board are some of our favorites. If you eat dairy, feel free to use whatever you like best.

Swap it!

Don't have Old Bay? Add 1 teaspoon of celery salt, ¼ teaspoon of paprika, ⅛ teaspoon of black pepper, and ⅛ teaspoon of mustard powder.

Kids in the Kitchen

Kids can mash the chickpeas and then mix in the other ingredients.

Sloppy Lentil Sandwiches

These sloppy sandwiches will transport you back to your childhood. The messier, the better. This recipe is just like the one I used to make before I went plant-based, but now I use healthy lentils instead of meat and they taste just as good, if not better. Put these on your menu tonight for a new family favorite meal!

2 tablespoons (28 ml) olive oil

¼ red onion, diced

1 green bell pepper, seeded and diced

2 small carrots, diced small or shredded

2 cloves garlic, minced

1 can (15 ounces, or 425 g) tomato sauce

¼ cup (60 g) ketchup

¼ cup (60 g) organic brown sugar

2 tablespoons (28 ml) vegan Worcestershire sauce

1–2 teaspoons liquid smoke (optional)

1 teaspoon yellow mustard

1 teaspoon dried oregano

¾ teaspoon salt, or to taste

¼ teaspoon black pepper, or to taste

2½ cups (495 g) cooked green or brown lentils

6 burger buns (gluten-free, if desired)

TOPPINGS OF CHOICE (OPTIONAL):

Tomatoes

Pickles

Avocado

Sliced onion

Yield: 6 servings

Heat the olive oil over medium heat in a large skillet. Add the onion, bell pepper, and carrots and sauté for 5 to 6 minutes until the onion is soft and translucent. Add the garlic and sauté for 1 minute.

Add the tomato sauce, ketchup, brown sugar, vegan Worcestershire sauce, liquid smoke (if using), yellow mustard, oregano, salt, and pepper. Increase the heat to bring to a low boil and then decrease the heat to low and simmer for 20 minutes.

Taste and adjust the seasoning, if necessary. Add the cooked lentils and stir until evenly coated. Simmer for another 10 minutes. Serve on buns with your choice of toppings.

TIP: You can often find packaged precooked lentils in the produce department of grocery stores. You might also find them in cans near the beans. They can be a real time-saver in this dish if you don't have leftover lentils in the fridge.

Smashed Black Bean Green Chile Quesadillas

Quesadillas are one of my go-to meals when I'm short on time and have nothing planned. Leftovers smashed in a tortilla and panfried until crisp instantly become a delicious dinner that everyone wants to eat. Bonus points if you serve it with a dipping sauce. No leftovers? No problem. Quesadillas don't require much work to make them taste amazing, even from scratch, like this recipe, which is super quick, flavorful, and kid-approved.

1 can (15 ounces, or 425 g) black beans, drained and rinsed

1 can (4.5 ounces, or 130 g) mild diced green chiles

1½ teaspoons cumin

1 teaspoon fine salt, or to taste

1 recipe Sharp Salsa Queso Dip (page 167)

5–6 flour tortillas (9 or 10 inches, or 23 or 26 cm each) (see note)

Cooking spray

Yield: 4 to 6 servings

In a small bowl, mix the black beans, green chiles, cumin, and salt. Using a potato masher or a fork, smash about half of the mixture. Set aside.

Lay one of the tortillas on a clean flat surface and spread 1 tablespoon (16 g) of Sharp Salsa Queso Dip on half of the tortilla, leaving a little space along the edge. Spread 3 tablespoons (45 g) of bean mixture over the top on the same side. Fold the other side over on top of the filling and press down gently to secure. Avoid pressing too hard as the filling will squish out. Repeat with the remaining tortillas.

Lightly spray a large nonstick skillet with cooking spray and heat over medium-high heat. Once hot, place two tortillas in the pan next to each other. Cook for 3 to 4 minutes until lightly browned and crispy on the bottom. Flip the quesadillas over and cook for another 2 to 3 minutes until the second side is also lightly browned.

Remove the quesadillas to a large plate or cutting board, in a single layer so they stay crispy. Repeat with the remaining quesadillas, spraying the pan again with cooking spray if it is dry. You may need to adjust the heat as you go, reducing the heat to medium if they are browning too much or too quickly.

Once the quesadillas have cooled slightly, slice each one in half or into fourths. Serve with the remaining Sharp Salsa Queso Dip on the side.

SERVING SUGGESTION: Serve with a simple green salad on the side to complete this meal.

Swap It!
You may use gluten-free tortillas if desired but note that corn tortillas don't bend well and may break.

Kids in the Kitchen
Have your kids mash the beans with the potato masher.

Black Bean Tacos
with Corn Radish Salsa and Pickled Red Onions

This is my go-to taco recipe. It's so easy, ready in twenty minutes or less, and made with pantry and fridge staples. Fresh summer sweet corn takes this recipe up a notch, but we make them all year round with thawed frozen corn and it's still crazy delicious.

FOR THE BLACK BEANS:

1 tablespoon (15 ml) olive oil

½ yellow onion, diced

1 tablespoon (8 g) chili powder

1 teaspoon cumin

2 cans (15 ounces, or 425 g each) black beans, drained and rinsed (or 3 cups [516 g] cooked beans)

½ cup (120 ml) low-sodium vegetable broth

¼ teaspoon salt, or to taste

Juice of ½ lime, or more to taste

FOR THE CORN RADISH SALSA:

1 cup (164 g) fresh or thawed corn kernels

2 radishes, diced (about ¼ cup [29 g])

½ jalapeño, diced (ribs and seeds removed)

Juice of ½ lime

½ teaspoon smoked paprika

¼ teaspoon cumin

¼ teaspoon salt, or to taste

FOR THE TACOS:

8 soft taco flour tortillas, warmed if desired (corn tortillas for gluten-free)

BEST Guacamole (page 162)

Quick Pickled Red Onions (page 170)

Yield: 4 servings, 2 tacos each

For the Black Beans: Heat the olive oil in a pot over medium heat. Add the onion and sauté for 4 to 5 minutes until soft and translucent. Add the chili powder and cumin and stir. Add the black beans and vegetable broth and simmer for 5 to 10 minutes. Using a potato masher or fork, mash about half of the bean mixture. Add the salt and lime juice. Taste and adjust the seasoning, if necessary. Remove from the heat.

For the Corn Radish Salsa: Add all the ingredients to a small bowl and mix well.

To assemble the tacos: Fill one tortilla with ¼ cup (43 g) of black beans, 2 tablespoons (32 g) of Corn Radish Salsa, a dollop of BEST Guacamole, and several Quick Pickled Red Onions. Repeat with the remaining tortillas.

TIP: Warm the tortillas! Place the stack of tortillas on a microwave-safe plate covered with a just-barely-damp paper towel. Microwave for 30 seconds at a time until warm. Alternatively, you can wrap the stack of tortillas in aluminum foil and warm in a preheated 350°F (180°C, or gas mark 4) oven for 10 to 15 minutes. Do this while you make the beans and everything will be ready at the same time.

Serving Suggestion
Serve with tortilla chips and more guacamole, of course!

Rice and Bean Pan-Grilled Burritos
with Avocado Green Chile Sauce

A burrito is essentially a taco's much larger and more filling brother. Tacos are generally served with sides to make a complete meal whereas a burrito is a complete meal in itself. Loaded with filling rice, protein-packed beans, fresh crunchy lettuce, and a swoon-worthy sauce, this is one meal that will surely leave you full and satisfied!

FOR THE RICE:

3 cups (585 g) cooked brown rice

¼ cup (4 g) chopped cilantro

1 medium tomato, diced

Juice of ½ lime

FOR THE BEANS:

1 tablespoon (15 ml) olive oil

2 teaspoons cumin

½ teaspoon smoked paprika

½ teaspoon chili powder

¼ teaspoon salt, or to taste

¼ teaspoon black pepper

1 can (15 ounces, or 425 g) pinto beans, drained and rinsed (or 1½ cups [257 g] cooked beans)

FOR THE AVOCADO GREEN CHILE SAUCE:

1 avocado, peel and pit removed

1 can (4.5 ounces, or 130 g) mild diced green chiles

Handful of cilantro

Juice of 2–3 limes

¾ teaspoon salt, or to taste

Water to thin, if needed

For the Rice: Mix the cooked brown rice with cilantro, tomato, and lime juice. Stir well.

For the Beans: In a small skillet, heat the olive oil over medium heat. Add the cumin, smoked paprika, chili powder, salt, and pepper and stir to make a slurry. Simmer, stirring occasionally, about 1 to 2 minutes until fragrant. Add the pinto beans, stir well, and cook for 2 to 3 minutes to heat through.

For the Avocado Green Chile Sauce: Add all the ingredients to a blender and purée until smooth.

To assemble the burritos: Wrap the tortillas in a just-damp paper towel and heat in the microwave for 20 to 30 seconds at a time until warm. Lay one tortilla flat and spread ¼ cup (50 g) of Avocado Green Chile Sauce horizontally on one end. Top with a scant one-sixth of rice mixture, ¼ cup (43 g) of beans, ¼ cup (12 g) of romaine lettuce, and a tablespoon or two (16 to 32 g) of salsa, if desired. Fold up the bottom half of the tortilla over the filling, then fold in both sides, and then starting from the bottom, tightly roll up the tortilla to form the burrito. Repeat with the remaining ingredients.

Swap It!
You may use gluten-free tortillas if desired but note that corn tortillas don't bend well and may break.

FOR THE BURRITOS:

1½ cups (71 g) chopped romaine lettuce

Salsa (optional)

6 large (10 inches, or 25 cm each) burrito-size flour tortillas

Cooking spray

Yield: 6 servings

Spray a skillet with cooking spray and heat over medium heat. Working in batches if needed, place the burritos seam-side down and cook for 3 to 4 minutes until lightly seared. The seam should stay closed once seared. Flip the burritos over and cook for another 3 to 4 minutes to sear the second side. You may need to adjust/lower the heat as you go. Watch them closely so they don't burn.

Cut each burrito in half and serve.

Smoky BBQ Burgers

This is a meaty burger that won't fall apart. There's BBQ sauce inside the burger for moisture and flavor, and of course, more BBQ sauce added on top of the burger makes this a family favorite! Serve it up with a side of fries.

2 teaspoons olive oil

½ cup (80 g) diced red onion (about ¼ large red onion)

1 clove garlic, minced

½ cup (50 g) raw walnuts

1 can (15 ounces, or 425 g) black beans, drained and rinsed (or 1½ cups [258 g] cooked beans)

1 cup (165 g) cooked rice (Leftover rice works great!)

1 teaspoon smoked paprika

¾ teaspoon fine salt

¼ teaspoon black pepper

¼ cup (60 ml) Sweet-and-Spicy BBQ sauce (page 165) or store-bought BBQ sauce, plus more for topping

¾ cup (38 g) panko or (30 g) bread crumbs (gluten-free, if desired)

4 burger buns (gluten-free, if desired)

Lettuce, mayo, pickles, etc., for topping

Yield: 4 burgers

These burgers can be panfried or oven-baked. If you are baking, preheat the oven to 350°F (180°C, or gas mark 4). Line a baking sheet with parchment paper and set aside.

Heat the olive oil in a small skillet over medium heat on the stove. Add the onion and garlic. Sauté for 5 to 6 minutes until soft and nearly all the liquid in the pan is gone. Turn off the heat.

In a food processor, pulse the walnuts until crumbly. Do not overprocess into flour, you want some small chunks for texture. Add the black beans, rice, sautéed onion and garlic, smoked paprika, salt, and pepper. Pulse just a few times until combined but still chunky.

Turn the mixture out into a large mixing bowl. Add the BBQ sauce and mix well with a spatula. Add the panko bread crumbs and mix well. You may need to get in there with your hands to mix and incorporate the bread crumbs evenly. The mixture should not be too sticky but should hold together well when pressed.

Divide the mixture in 4 sections. Form each section into a patty about 3 to 3½ inches (7.5 to 8.5 cm) in diameter.

If baking, place the patties on the prepared baking sheet. Bake for 15 minutes, gently flip over, and bake for 10 more minutes. Let sit for 5 minutes before serving.

If panfrying, spritz a skillet lightly with cooking spray and heat over medium heat. Place the patties in the pan with space in between each one. Cook for 10 to 15 minutes, gently flip over, and cook for another 10 to 15 minutes more. You may need to adjust the heat as you go if you find they are browning too quickly.

Serve on buns with more BBQ sauce and any toppings you desire.

TIP: Don't have a food processor? No problem. Finely chop the walnuts with a sharp knife and mash the beans with a potato masher or fork. Mix everything together well in a mixing bowl.

NOTE: You could also make these into 6 to 8 slider-size burgers.

CHAPTER 5

Bountiful Bowls

Bowls are a staple of meatless cooking. It's the perfect vessel for combining several ingredients into one composed dish. Bowls are ideal for picky eaters who want to customize their own, as most components are kept separate until added to individual bowls. Letting kids choose their own additions to the bowl makes them feel in charge and increases the chance of them trying something new. Kids may also prefer the sauce on the side instead of drizzled over the top of the bowl.

Buffalo Cauliflower Bowls
with Avocado Crema

Who doesn't love buffalo sauce? It's spicy and tangy and so delicious! If you're worried about the heat, the so-good-you'll-want-to-eat-it-by-the-spoonful Avocado Crema is going to help to cool things down.

FOR THE BUFFALO CAULIFLOWER:

1 head cauliflower, cut into florets (about 4–5 cups [500–600 g])

1 tablespoon (15 ml) olive oil

1 teaspoon salt

¼ teaspoon garlic powder

¼ teaspoon black pepper

½ cup (120 ml) buffalo style hot sauce (We like Frank's Red Hot but use your favorite.)

FOR THE AVOCADO CREMA:

1 avocado, peel and pit removed

1 container (5.5 ounces, or 155 g) plain plant-based yogurt

Juice of ½ lime

½ teaspoon salt, or to taste

FOR THE BOWLS:

2 cups (370 g) cooked quinoa

4 cups (400 g) coleslaw mix

¼ cup (4 g) chopped cilantro

Yield: 4 servings

Preheat the oven to 450°F (230°C, or gas mark 8). Lightly spray a rimmed baking sheet with cooking spray and set aside.

For the For the Buffalo Cauliflower: In a large mixing bowl, combine the cauliflower florets, olive oil, salt, garlic powder, and pepper. Mix well to coat evenly. Spread the cauliflower out onto the prepared baking sheet in one even layer. Try to leave a little room between the florets if possible. Roast for 15 minutes.

Pour the buffalo hot sauce into the same mixing bowl you used before. Add the roasted cauliflower and mix well to evenly coat. Spread out onto the baking sheet again in one even layer and roast for another 5 to 10 minutes until just tender.

For the Avocado Crema: Add all the ingredients to a blender or food processor and purée until smooth.

To build your bowls: Add ½ cup (92 g) of quinoa to each bowl with 1 cup (100 g) of coleslaw mix, one-quarter of the roasted buffalo cauliflower, 1 tablespoon (1 g) of cilantro, and a few tablespoons (around 45 g) of Avocado Crema.

TIP: If your kids (or you) aren't keen on spicy, only coat half of the cauliflower in the buffalo sauce and shake off any excess before returning it to the baking sheet.

Mediterranean Quinoa Bowls
with Roasted Chickpeas

These bowls make me feel healthier just by looking at them: superfood quinoa, protein-packed chickpeas, nutritional powerhouse greens, and vibrantly fresh cucumber-tomato salad. The Citrus Tahini Dressing is the perfect creamy sauce to bring it all together.

FOR THE ROASTED CHICKPEAS:

1 can (15 ounces, or 425 g) chickpeas, drained, rinsed, and patted dry

1 teaspoon cumin

½ teaspoon dried oregano

¼ teaspoon ground turmeric

¼ teaspoon garlic powder

¼ teaspoon salt

1 teaspoon olive oil

FOR THE QUINOA:

1 tablespoon (15 ml) olive oil

1 cup (173 g) dry quinoa, rinsed well with cold water

1½ cups (355 ml) low-sodium vegetable broth

Salt and black pepper

FOR THE BOWLS:

1 English cucumber, diced

1 pint (275 g) grape tomatoes, halved

¼ red onion, diced

3–4 tablespoons (12–15 g) chopped fresh parsley

Juice of 1 lemon

¼–½ teaspoon salt, or to taste

4 cups (220 g) baby salad greens

1 recipe Citrus Tahini Dressing (page 163)

Yield: 4 servings

For the Roasted Chickpeas: Preheat the oven to 400°F (200°C, or gas mark 6). Line a rimmed baking sheet with parchment paper and set aside.

Toss the chickpeas in a bowl with the spices and olive oil; mix well. Spread them out onto the prepared baking sheet in an even layer. Roast for 15 minutes, stir the chickpeas, and roast for 10 to 15 more minutes until browning and crunchy. They will continue to crisp up as they cool.

For the Quinoa: Heat the oil in a pot over medium heat on the stove. Add the quinoa and sauté for 2 to 3 minutes to toast, stirring frequently to prevent burning. Carefully add the vegetable broth. Increase the heat to high and bring to a boil, cover, and then reduce the heat to low. Simmer for 10 to 15 minutes until tender. Add salt and pepper, if desired, to taste.

While the quinoa is cooking, toss the cucumbers, tomatoes, onion, parsley, lemon, and salt in a bowl. Mix well. Taste and adjust the seasoning, if needed.

To assemble the bowls: Place 1 cup (55 g) of salad greens in the bottom of a bowl. Top it with ¾ cup (139 g) of quinoa, one-quarter of the cucumber-tomato salad, one-quarter of the roasted chickpeas, and 2 to 3 tablespoons (28 to 45 ml) of the Citrus Tahini Dressing.

Pineapple Curried Cauliflower Rice Bowls

Are you cutting back on grains? This one is for you. Shredded cauliflower brilliantly stands in for rice in this dish. Bright, sweet pineapple balances the earthiness of the curry perfectly. I use canned pineapple here for convenience all year long, but feel free to use fresh if it's in season.

FOR THE CHICKPEAS:

1 can (15 ounces, or 425 g) chickpeas, drained and rinsed

1 teaspoon olive oil

Salt and black pepper

FOR THE CURRIED CAULIFLOWER RICE:

1 head cauliflower, broken into florets

1 tablespoon (14 g) coconut oil or (15 ml) olive oil

1 yellow onion, diced

1 red bell pepper, seeded and diced

1 cup (110 g) shredded carrots

2 teaspoons yellow curry powder

1 teaspoon garlic powder

¾ teaspoon salt

1 cup (130 g) frozen green peas

1 can (20 ounces, or 560 g) pineapple chunks, drained

FOR SERVING:

¼ cup (35 g) raw shelled pumpkin seeds

¼ cup (4 g) chopped cilantro

Yield: 4 servings

For the Chickpeas: Preheat the oven to 400°F (200°C, or gas mark 6).

Toss the chickpeas with olive oil, salt, and pepper and spread out onto a rimmed baking sheet in one even layer. Bake for 25 to 30 minutes, shaking the pan every 10 minutes to toss the chickpeas. Set aside. The chickpeas will continue to crisp up while they sit.

For the Curried Cauliflower Rice: Working in 2 to 3 batches, pulse the cauliflower in a food processor, stopping to scrape down the sides as necessary, until the texture resembles rice. Do not overprocess! You should have about 4 cups (400 g) of riced cauliflower. Set aside.

Heat the coconut oil in a large pan over medium heat on the stove. Add the onion and sauté for 5 to 6 minutes until soft and translucent. Add the bell pepper and carrots and sauté for 5 to 6 minutes until starting to soften. Add the curry powder, garlic powder, and salt and sauté for 1 minute until fragrant. Add the riced cauliflower and sauté for 7 to 8 minutes, stirring occasionally to prevent sticking. Add the green peas and pineapple chunks, stir to combine, and sauté for 2 to 3 minutes to heat through.

To assemble the bowls: Divide the mixture among 4 bowls and top with one-quarter of the roasted chickpeas. Sprinkle with 1 tablespoon (about 9 g) of pumpkin seeds and 1 tablespoon (1 g) of cilantro.

Brown Rice Bowls
with Roasted Veggies and Chickpeas

This is a classic grains, veggies, protein, and sauce bowl. It's all our favorites in one bowl drizzled with the most amazing sweet tahini sauce. The whole thing comes together quickly and easily, and everyone will clean their plates!

1 cup (190 g) brown rice

1 head cauliflower, cut into bite-size florets

1 head broccoli, cut into bite-size florets

1 can (15 ounces, or 425 g) chickpeas (or 1½ cups [246 g] cooked chickpeas)

3 medium carrots, cut into coins

2 tablespoons sesame seeds

2 teaspoons olive oil

Salt and black pepper

FOR THE CREAMY SWEET TAHINI DRESSING:

¼ cup (60 g) tahini

3 tablespoons (45 ml) balsamic vinegar

2 tablespoons (40 g) pure maple syrup

1 clove garlic, minced

3 tablespoons (12 g) nutritional yeast

¼ cup (60 ml) water, plus more as needed to thin

Salt and black pepper

Yield: 4 servings

Preheat the oven to 400°F (200°C, or gas mark 6). Line 2 rimmed baking sheets with parchment paper and set aside.

Cook the rice according to package directions.

Spread the cauliflower and broccoli on one baking sheet. Spread the chickpeas and carrots on another baking sheet. Drizzle 1 teaspoon of olive oil over each baking sheet and give the veggies a toss. Sprinkle with salt and pepper.

Roast for 20 to 30 minutes, turning the pans and giving them a shake every 10 minutes. The cauliflower and broccoli take about 30 minutes and the carrots and chickpeas take about 20, so start the broccoli/cauliflower first and put the chickpeas/carrots in after the first 10 minutes. Every oven is different, so keep an eye on everything to make sure you don't burn them.

For the Creamy Sweet Tahini Dressing: Combine all the ingredients in a small bowl or cup and whisk until smooth. Add more water to thin, as needed. Taste and adjust seasoning. Set aside.

When veggies and chickpeas are done, make your bowls! Add a little rice, broccoli, cauliflower, carrots, chickpeas, sesame seeds, and Creamy Sweet Tahini Dressing in each individual bowl.

TIP: Use quick-cook brown rice. It only takes 10 to 15 minutes!

Fried Rice Bowls with Baked Tofu

Throw away your carry-out menus and make this easy homemade fried rice bowl instead! It's so much healthier than restaurant versions, but just as satisfying.

3 tablespoons (45 ml) tamari, coconut aminos, or soy sauce (gluten-free, if desired)

¼ cup (63 g) hoisin sauce

3 tablespoons (45 ml) rice wine vinegar

3 cloves garlic, minced

2 teaspoons ground ginger

A few shakes of sriracha (optional)

1 tablespoon (15 ml) peanut oil

1 cup (90 g) chopped cabbage

½ red bell pepper, seeded and diced

1 cup (63 g) snow peas, halved

3 scallions, diced

½ cup (65 g) sweet green peas

4 cups (780 g) leftover cooked brown rice

1 recipe Addictive Tofu, either version (page 168)

1–2 teaspoons sesame oil (optional)

2–3 tablespoons (16–24 g) white sesame seeds

Yield: 6 servings

Whisk together the tamari, hoisin, rice wine vinegar, garlic, ginger, and sriracha (if using) in a small bowl or measuring cup and set aside.

Heat the peanut oil in a skillet over medium-high heat, add the cabbage, bell pepper and snow peas. Cook for 2 to 3 minutes, stirring frequently, until just starting to soften. You want the veggies to retain their fresh flavor and still give a nice crunch, so don't overcook!

Add the scallions and sweet peas and cook for 1 minute while stirring. Add the sauce to the veggies and stir to coat. Add the rice and stir until evenly coated in the sauce. Continue cooking for 3 to 4 minutes to heat through.

To serve, divide the fried rice among 6 bowls. Top with Addictive Tofu and a few more dashes of sriracha if you like the heat. Drizzle with sesame oil, if using, and sprinkle with sesame seeds.

NOTE: Hoisin sauce is an Asian barbecue sauce. It's thick and savory with a hint of sweet and spicy. It brings so much flavor with very little effort. You can usually find hoisin sauce near the Asian noodles and soy sauces in your grocery store. A small jar should only cost a couple dollars.

Add It or Swap It!

This dish is easy to customize. Use green beans instead of snow peas or shredded carrots instead of bell peppers. Or add those extra veggies in addition to the others. If you increase the amount of vegetables used, decrease the amount of rice to ensure there is enough sauce to coat the dish.

Sticky Orange Tofu Bowls

This dish will remind you of your favorite take-out, but it's much healthier as you control the ingredients. The sticky sweet orange sauce is loaded with diced peppers, and it's ready in under thirty minutes.

1 recipe Addictive Tofu, either version (page 168)

1 tablespoon (15 ml) olive oil

½ red onion, diced

3 cloves garlic, minced

2 sweet bell peppers, seeded and diced

1½ cups (355 ml) fresh orange juice

¼ cup (60 ml) tamari, coconut aminos, or soy sauce (gluten-free, if desired)

3 tablespoons (60 g) pure maple syrup

3 tablespoons (45 ml) unseasoned rice vinegar

2 tablespoons (16 g) cornstarch

¼ cup (60 ml) water

4 cups (660 g) cooked rice

Sliced scallions

Sprinkle of sesame seeds

Yield: 4 servings

Make the Addictive Tofu and set aside.

Wipe down the same skillet, add the olive oil, and heat on the stove over medium heat. Add the onion and sauté for 5 to 6 minutes until soft and translucent. Add the garlic and bell peppers and sauté for 5 to 6 minutes until they start to soften.

Add the orange juice, tamari, maple syrup, and rice vinegar to the skillet and stir to combine.

In a small bowl, whisk the cornstarch and water until smooth. Add it to the skillet, increase the heat to high to bring to a boil, and then reduce the heat to medium-low. Simmer for 15 to 20 minutes until thick and glossy.

Divide the rice among 4 bowls. Pour ¾ cup (175 ml) of the sauce over the rice and one-quarter of the Addictive Tofu on top. Garnish with scallions and a sprinkle of sesame seeds.

TIP: The tofu can be made ahead of time and kept in the fridge for 2 to 3 days until ready to use. It can also be added to the sauce before serving if you prefer. I like to keep it separate so the kids can choose how much sauce versus tofu they add to their bowls.

Serving Suggestion

Roasted cauliflower makes a great addition to this dish or a replacement for the Addictive Tofu.

Easiest Rice and Beans Bowls

I've been making this dish since the days when I was living in my first apartment in downtown Chicago. Short on funds and with little motivation to cook, this was my go-to meal. I'd cook once and eat all week. If you can even call it cooking—it's more like heating. But don't knock it, because it's delicious! It's still one of my go-to meals because it's a family favorite. It proves that you don't need a lot of time or money to enjoy a healthy plant-based meal!

2 cups (390 g) cooked brown rice

1 can (15 ounces, or 425 g) black beans, drained and rinsed

2 cups (328 g) fresh or frozen corn kernels

1 jar (12 ounces, or 340 g) tomato-based salsa

1 red bell pepper, seeded and diced

Handful of cilantro, chopped

1 recipe BEST Guacamole (page 162)

Tortilla chips, for serving

Yield: 4 servings

Combine the rice, black beans, corn, and salsa in a skillet over medium heat. Cook, stirring occasionally until heated through, about 5 to 10 minutes. Take off the heat, add the bell pepper and cilantro, and stir to combine.

Divide among 4 bowls and top with a big dollop of BEST Guacamole. Serve with tortilla chips for dipping.

NOTE: If you don't have leftover rice, use instant brown rice that cooks in 5 to 10 minutes for a super easy 20-minute dinner.

Swap It!
Skip the chips and serve it over chopped romaine lettuce for a healthy salad version.

Kids in the Kitchen
The kids may need your help cutting the bell pepper, but they can probably make the rest on their own—dumping the ingredients in the skillet and stirring.

BBQ Chickpea and Veggie Bowls

This is another version of a grains, beans, and veggies bowl. These roasted vegetables are so good, in our house, the kids are eating them off the hot-from-the-oven pan. We're lucky if we have enough left to make our bowls. I'm not complaining! With sticky BBQ sauce and addictive roasted vegetables, this dish is a winner!

1 can (15 ounces, or 425 g) chickpeas, drained and rinsed

1 head broccoli, chopped into bite-size florets

2 red bell peppers, seeded and sliced (or color of your choice)

1 red onion, halved and sliced

2 tablespoons (28 ml) olive oil

¼ teaspoon salt, or to taste

¼ teaspoon black pepper, or to taste

2 cups (390 g) cooked brown rice

1 avocado, peel and pit removed, diced

¼ cup (4 g) cilantro, chopped

1 cup (235 ml) Sweet-and-Spicy BBQ Sauce (page 165) or store-bought BBQ sauce

Yield: 4 servings

Preheat the oven to 375°F (190°C, or gas mark 5). Line 2 rimmed baking sheets with parchment paper.

Spread out the chickpeas, broccoli, bell peppers, and onion on the baking sheet. Drizzle with olive oil, sprinkle with salt and pepper, and toss to coat. Spread them out in one even layer. Roast for 20 minutes, mix the veggies, and swap the pans in the oven so the one on top is now on the bottom. Roast for another 10 to 15 minutes until the veggies are starting to char and the chickpeas are crispy (they will continue to crisp up as they sit).

Add ½ cup (98 g) of cooked rice to each of 4 bowls. Divvy up the roasted vegetables, diced avocado, and cilantro equally among the bowls. Drizzle with the BBQ sauce.

Swap It!

Try this recipe with Addictive Chewy Baked Tofu (page 168) instead of the chickpeas. Or, swap in cauliflower for the broccoli, if you prefer.

Jimbo's Red Beans and Rice Bowls

This recipe comes from my friend Jim, who is married to one of my best friends. Jim also happens to be a chef in a prominent downtown Chicago restaurant, although he hails from Louisiana, which is where this Cajun dish comes into play. I asked Jim if he had any recipe suggestions for this cookbook and Red Beans and Rice came up right away. It fits in perfectly with the style of this cookbook: easy, family-friendly, loaded with veggies, and delicious! I took Jim's recipe and made it my own, but you have him to thank for most of it!

2 tablespoons (28 ml) olive oil

1 yellow onion, diced

3 ribs celery, diced

1 large green pepper, seeded and diced

2 cloves garlic, minced

2 teaspoons Italian seasoning

¾ teaspoon garlic salt

½ teaspoon onion powder

1¼ teaspoons salt, or to taste

½ teaspoon black pepper, or to taste

3 cans (15 ounces, or 425 g each) red kidney beans, drained and rinsed

1–2 tablespoons (15–28 ml) liquid smoke

2–4 tablespoons (28–60 ml) hot pepper sauce (We like Frank's Red Hot because it has a tangy sweet heat.)

1¼ cups (285 ml) low-sodium vegetable broth

3 cups (474 g) cooked long-grain white rice

2 scallions, sliced (optional)

Yield: 6 servings

Heat the olive oil in a large skillet over medium heat. Add the onion and sauté for 5 to 6 minutes until soft and translucent. Add the celery, green pepper, and garlic and sauté for 5 to 6 minutes until starting to soften.

Add the Italian seasoning, garlic salt, onion powder, salt, and pepper, stir to combine, and cook for 1 minute.

Add the kidney beans, 1 tablespoon (15 ml) of liquid smoke, 2 tablespoons (28 ml) of hot sauce, and vegetable broth. Bring to a boil and then to reduce the heat to medium-low and simmer for 20 minutes, stirring occasionally.

Taste and adjust the seasoning, if necessary. Add additional salt, pepper, liquid smoke, and hot pepper sauce according to your family's tastes.

Serve over rice with a garnish of scallions, if using.

Serving Suggestion

A thick slice of cornbread is the perfect accompaniment to this rice bowl.

Red Lentil Chickpea Cacciatore Bowls

This cacciatore sauce is a big winner among my kids. They unanimously told me I should add this recipe to the cookbook after trying it for the first time. They like it with spaghetti noodles and chickpeas. I prefer it over rice with Addictive Chewy Baked Tofu (page 168). Use whatever sounds good to you!

12 ounces (340 g) spaghetti noodles or noodles of choice (gluten-free, if desired)

2 tablespoons (28 ml) olive oil

1 yellow onion, diced

1 carrot, peeled and diced

2 cloves garlic, minced

2 tablespoons (32 g) tomato paste

1 tablespoon (6 g) Italian seasoning

1 teaspoon dried oregano

¼ teaspoon black pepper, or to taste

1 red bell pepper, seeded and sliced thin

1 yellow or orange bell pepper, seeded and sliced thin

½ cup (96 g) dry red lentils, picked over and rinsed well in cold water

2 cans (14.5 ounces, or 410 g each) diced tomatoes

1½ cups (355 ml) low-sodium vegetable broth

1 can (15 ounces, or 425 g) chickpeas, drained and rinsed

1 teaspoon salt, or to taste

2 tablespoons (28 ml) red wine vinegar

¼ cup (15 g) chopped fresh parsley

Yield: 4 to 6 servings

Cook the noodles according to package directions.

Meanwhile, heat the olive oil in a large skillet over medium heat. Add the onion and carrot and sauté for 5 to 6 minutes until soft and translucent. Add the garlic and sauté for 1 minute. Add the tomato paste, Italian seasoning, oregano, and pepper. Sauté for 1 to 2 minutes until fragrant and the tomato paste is incorporated.

Add the bell peppers, red lentils, tomatoes, and vegetable broth. Increase the heat to high to bring to a boil, then cover and reduce the heat to medium-low. Simmer for 15 to 20 minutes until the lentils are tender.

Add the chickpeas, salt, red wine vinegar, and parsley and stir to combine. Cook for another 2 to 3 minutes to heat through.

To serve, add a portion of noodles to a bowl and top with a portion of the cacciatore sauce.

Swap It!
You could serve this with ½ cup (82 g) of cooked rice per person instead of noodles, if you prefer.

Feel free to swap out the chickpeas for Addictive Crispy Panfried Tofu (page 168) instead.

Roasted Winter Vegetable Bowls
with Couscous, Romesco Sauce, and Tahini Drizzle

This is one of my favorite recipes in this book. The combination of flavors and textures exceeded my expectations, and now I find myself craving a big bowl. It may seem like a lot of steps, but they are all easy and can basically be done at the same time. The romesco sauce can be made ahead of time and kept in the fridge. Have the kids whisk up the dressing to save you one extra step.

FOR THE ROASTED VEGETABLES:

2 sweet potatoes, peeled and chopped into 1-inch (2.5 cm) cubes

2 parsnips, peeled and chopped into 1-inch (2.5 cm) cubes

8 radishes, halved or quartered if large

1 red onion, halved and sliced

1 tablespoon (15 ml) olive oil

1 teaspoon dried thyme

¼ teaspoon salt, or to taste

⅛ teaspoon black pepper, or to taste

FOR THE COUSCOUS:

1½ cups (355 ml) water

1 teaspoon olive oil

¼ teaspoon salt, or to taste

1 cup (175 g) dry couscous

FOR THE SPICY TOASTED PUMPKIN SEEDS:

½ cup (70 g) raw shelled pumpkin seeds

1 teaspoon olive oil

1 teaspoon pure maple syrup

¼ teaspoon cayenne

¼ teaspoon garlic powder

For the Roasted Vegetables: Preheat the oven to 400°F (200°C, or gas mark 6). Line a rimmed baking sheet with parchment paper and set aside.

Place all the ingredients in a large mixing bowl and toss well. Spread out onto the prepared baking sheet in one even layer. Roast for 15 minutes, stir vegetables and spread back out in one even layer and then roast for 10 to 15 minutes more.

For the Couscous: Bring the water to a boil, turn off the heat, and add the olive oil and salt. Pour in the couscous and let it sit for 5 to 10 minutes. When all the water is absorbed, fluff with a fork. Stirring with a spoon may create clumps; a fork is best here.

For the Spicy Toasted Pumpkin Seeds: Line a small plate with parchment paper and set aside. Heat the olive oil, maple syrup, cayenne, and garlic powder in a small skillet over medium heat, stirring gently. When you start to see it sizzling, add the pumpkin seeds. Stir frequently until the seeds are toasted, about 4 to 5 minutes. Transfer the pumpkin seeds to the prepared plate. They will continue to crisp up as they sit.

Swap It!

Make this dish gluten-free by using 1 cup (173 g) of quinoa, cooked according to package directions, in place of the couscous.

FOR THE TAHINI DRIZZLE:

⅓ cup (80 g) tahini

1 tablespoon (20 g) pure maple syrup

1 tablespoon (15 ml) balsamic vinegar

FOR THE BOWLS:

4 cups (120 g) baby spinach

1 recipe Romesco Sauce (page 166)

1 recipe Tahini Drizzle (see below)

2–4 tablespoons (28–60 ml) water, to thin

Yield: 4 servings

For the Tahini Drizzle: Add the tahini, maple syrup, and balsamic vinegar to a small bowl. Stir to combine. Add water 1 tablespoon (15 ml) at a time until desired consistency is reached.

To assemble the bowls: Place 1 cup (30 g) of baby spinach in a bowl, top with one-quarter of the couscous, one-quarter of the roasted vegetables, a generous dollop of Romesco sauce, 2 tablespoons (18 g) of Spicy Toasted Pumpkin Seeds, and a tablespoon or two of Tahini Drizzle.

TIP: While the vegetables are roasting, you can make all other components of the dish so that everything is ready to go when the vegetables are done.

NOTE: Don't be afraid of the cayenne in the Spicy Toasted Pumpkin Seeds. The seeds will taste spicy right out of the skillet, but when eaten with the other bowl ingredients, the flavors will complement each other and tone down the spiciness.

CHAPTER 6

Perfect Pasta

I've never met anyone who doesn't love pasta—and it's the magical ingredient that brings kids to the table time and time again. Pasta is quick, easy, and incredibly versatile. It can stand alone or be used in soups and salads. It's the secret to turning basic ingredients into a meal.

Pasta with Eggplant in Tomato Cream Sauce

Eggplant doesn't have to be peeled, but I find the skin to be a bit tough sometimes. Once peeled, you're left with a sponge that soaks up all the yummy flavors you throw its way. In this dish, it becomes "meaty" and filling. This recipe reminds me of a dish I used to get at Maggiano's Little Italy many, many years ago. I searched their menu online while writing this book, but it doesn't look like they serve it anymore. Good thing we have this version!

FOR THE CASHEW CREAM:

1 cup (140 g) raw cashews, soaked in hot water for at least 30 minutes

1 cup (235 ml) water

FOR THE PASTA AND EGGPLANT:

12 ounces (340 g) rigatoni or penne (gluten-free, if desired)

2 tablespoons (28 ml) olive oil

½ yellow onion, diced

2 cloves garlic, minced

1 globe eggplant, peeled and chopped into 1-inch (2.5 cm) pieces (about 4 cups [328 g] chopped)

1 teaspoon dried oregano

½ teaspoon dried basil

¼ teaspoon crushed red pepper flakes, or more to taste

1 can (28 ounces, or 785 g) crushed tomatoes

½ cup (120 ml) low-sodium vegetable broth

1 teaspoon organic white sugar

1 teaspoon salt, or to taste

½ teaspoon black pepper

1 teaspoon balsamic vinegar

½ cup Cashew Cream (recipe below)

Big handful of baby spinach

Yield: 4 servings

For the Cashew Cream: Add the soaked cashews and water to a high-speed blender and blend until smooth. Reserve ½ cup (120 ml) and store the rest in an airtight container in the fridge for 3 to 4 days. You can use it just like you would heavy cream or half and half.

For the Pasta and Eggplant: Cook the pasta according to package directions.

Meanwhile, heat the olive oil in a large deep skillet over medium heat. Add the onion and sauté for 4 to 5 minutes until soft and translucent. Add the garlic and sauté for 1 minute.

Add the eggplant, oregano, basil, and crushed red pepper flakes. Cook for 5 minutes until the eggplant is starting to soften. Add the crushed tomatoes, vegetable broth, sugar, salt, and pepper and simmer for 15 to 20 minutes.

Add the balsamic vinegar and ½ cup (120 ml) of Cashew Cream and stir well to combine. Add the spinach and stir until it starts to wilt a bit, about 1 to 2 minutes.

Serve the sauce over the noodles.

NOTE: Cashew Cream is easier to make in a large batch, which is why we are making more than we need. Add the remainder to soups and sauces, drizzle it over casseroles, or add a bit of powdered sugar and drizzle it on oatmeal, pancakes, or granola bars as "icing."

Lentil Bolognese with Spaghetti

This one of my go-to meals. The kids love anything served with spaghetti noodles, and I love that it contains healthy plant-based protein and fiber. I occasionally leave out the mushrooms because my son genuinely doesn't care for them, but if I chop them small enough, he usually doesn't even notice.

16 ounces (455 g) spaghetti noodles or pasta of choice (gluten-free, if desired)

1 tablespoon (15 ml) olive oil

½ sweet onion, diced

10 ounces (280 g) cremini mushrooms, finely diced

¼ cup (60 ml) robust dry red wine

1 can (28 ounces, or 785 g) crushed tomatoes

½ cup (120 ml) low-sodium vegetable broth

2 tablespoons (28 ml) balsamic vinegar

1 tablespoon (15 ml) tamari, coconut aminos, or soy sauce (gluten-free, if desired)

2 tablespoons (2 g) dried parsley

1 tablespoon (5 g) dried basil

2 teaspoons dried oregano

1 teaspoon salt, or to taste

¼ teaspoon black pepper, or to taste

1 cup (198 g) cooked brown or green lentils

Yield: 6 servings

Cook the spaghetti according to package directions.

Heat the olive oil over medium heat in a large skillet. Add the onion and sauté until soft and translucent, about 5 to 6 minutes. Add the mushrooms and sauté for 7 to 8 minutes until soft and cooked through, stirring occasionally.

Add the wine and sauté until no liquid is left, stirring occasionally. Add the crushed tomatoes, vegetable broth, balsamic vinegar, tamari, parsley, basil, oregano, salt, and pepper. Stir to combine. Reduce heat to medium-low and simmer for 15 minutes. Add the cooked lentils and stir to combine. Cook for another 2 to 3 minutes to heat through.

Serve warm over the spaghetti.

SERVING SUGGESTION: Serve with a simple salad and garlic bread to complete the meal.

Swap It!

If you want to avoid alcohol, you can leave out the wine.

Vegan Scampi in Lemon Garlic White Wine Sauce

This is a really simple dish that tastes elegant. Hearts of palm are the perfect stand-in for scallops. They have a similar look when sliced and a briny quality reminiscent of seafood—great for those with a shellfish allergy.

3 tablespoons (45 ml) olive oil, divided

1 jar (14.8 ounces, or 420 g) hearts of palm

½ teaspoon salt, divided

¼ teaspoon black pepper, divided

8 ounces (225 g) linguine or pasta of choice (gluten-free, if desired)

4 cloves garlic, minced

½ cup (120 ml) dry white wine

Juice of 1 lemon

1 cup (235 ml) low-sodium vegetable broth

Handful of fresh parsley, chopped

Pinch of crushed red pepper flakes (optional)

2 tablespoons (6 g) panko bread crumbs (gluten-free, if desired)

1 tablespoon (4 g) nutritional yeast (optional)

Yield: 4 servings

Fill a large pasta pot with water and bring to a boil.

Meanwhile, carefully slice the hearts of palm crosswise into ½-inch (1 cm) slices.

Heat 1 tablespoon (15 ml) of olive oil in a large skillet over medium-high heat. Once the oil is hot, add the hearts of palm. Sprinkle with ¼ teaspoon of salt and ⅛ teaspoon of pepper. Sear until gold brown, about 2 to 3 minutes. Gently flip each slice over. Sprinkle with the remaining ¼ teaspoon of salt and ⅛ teaspoon of pepper. Sear for another 2 to 3 minutes until golden brown. Transfer to a plate.

Drop the pasta in the boiling water and cook according to package directions.

Meanwhile, heat the remaining 2 tablespoons (28 ml) of olive oil over medium heat. Sauté the garlic for 1 to 2 minutes. Add the white wine and simmer for 3 to 4 minutes until the liquid reduces by about half. Add the lemon juice and vegetable broth and simmer for 5 minutes until reduced and glossy.

Add the cooked pasta to the skillet and toss to combine. Add the seared hearts of palm to the skillet along with the parsley and crushed red pepper flakes.

Stir together the panko bread crumbs and the nutritional yeast, if using. Sprinkle over the pasta and toss everything to combine.

Swap It!

Are you avoiding alcohol? Use the same amount of vegetable broth with 2 tablespoons (28 ml) of white wine vinegar.

Kids in the Kitchen

Have your kids stir the bread crumbs and nutritional yeast together and sprinkle it over the pasta.

Butternut Squash Mac and Cheese

Macaroni noodles are drenched in a creamy, cheesy pasta sauce with hidden veggies that no one will detect. It's a family favorite that happens to be the #1 most viewed and remade recipe on my blog. It even survived a kids' taste test on national TV. Spoiler alert: They all loved it!

1 recipe Butternut Mac Cheese Sauce (page 167)

12 ounces (340 g) macaroni noodles (gluten-free, if desired)

Yield: 4 to 6 servings

Make the Butternut Mac Cheese Sauce according to directions.

Cook the macaroni noodles according to package directions. Add the pasta back to the pot.

Add the Butternut Mac Cheese Sauce to the pasta and stir well to combine.

Add It!

Frozen peas are a great addition. Simply add them to the strainer and drain the pasta over them. Fresh spinach would also work great.

Rigatoni with Romesco and Broccoli

It doesn't get much easier than this. Make the Romesco Sauce while the pasta water comes to a boil. Chop the broccoli into florets during the first few minutes of pasta cooking time. Combine and eat! The smoky Spanish-inspired Romesco Sauce is a nice change of pace from typical marinara flavors.

12 ounces (340 g) rigatoni pasta, or other tube-shaped pasta

2 cups (142 g) broccoli florets

1 recipe Romesco Sauce (page 166)

Salt and black pepper

Yield: 4 servings

Cook the pasta according to package directions, making sure to salt the cooking water well. When there is 4 minutes left for the pasta, add the broccoli florets to the pasta water. Drain the pasta and broccoli together when done. Add back to the pot, pour in the Romesco Sauce, and stir to ensure everything is evenly coated.

Season with salt and pepper, if desired.

Kids in the Kitchen

Have your kids make the romesco sauce and break the broccoli into florets.

Buttered Noodles
with Roasted Cauliflower and Seedy Bread Crumbs

What kid doesn't love buttered noodles? Speaking of kids, growing up we ate a lot of steamed cauliflower with bread crumbs. I'd drizzle it with malt vinegar and it was one of my favorite side dishes. I decided to combine these two childhood memories and give it a healthy twist with hemp seeds and pumpkin seeds (pepitas). Here the cauliflower is roasted, not steamed, to bring out its flavor. The seeds are pulverized to resemble bread crumbs. Kids and adults alike will want seconds.

1 small head cauliflower, chopped into bite-size florets

2 tablespoons (28 ml) olive oil, divided

¾ teaspoon salt, divided

¼ teaspoon black pepper

¼ teaspoon garlic powder

8 ounces (225 g) spaghetti noodles or pasta of choice (gluten-free, if desired)

¼ cup (37 g) hemp seeds

¼ cup (35 g) raw shelled pumpkin seeds (pepitas)

4 cloves garlic, minced

3 tablespoons (42 g) plant-based butter

Pinch of crushed red pepper flakes (optional)

Vegetable broth, as needed to loosen the pasta

Yield: 4 to 6 servings

Preheat the oven to 450°F (230°C, or gas mark 8). Line a rimmed baking sheet with parchment paper and set aside.

Toss the cauliflower florets with 1 tablespoon (15 ml) of olive oil, ½ teaspoon of salt, pepper, and garlic powder. Spread out onto the prepared baking sheet in one even layer. Bake for 15 minutes or until tender and the edges are golden brown.

Meanwhile, cook the spaghetti according to package directions. Reserve 1 cup (235 ml) of the pasta cooking water before draining.

While the pasta is cooking, add the hemp seeds and pumpkin seeds and remaining ¼ teaspoon salt to a food processor. Pulse until combined and the mixture resembles a fine crumb. Set aside.

Meanwhile, heat the remaining 1 tablespoon (15 ml) of olive oil in a large skillet over medium heat. Add the garlic and sauté for 3 to 4 minutes until fragrant. Add the butter and sauté until melted. Add the crushed red pepper flakes, if using.

Add the drained spaghetti to the skillet and toss well to coat. Add the reserved 1 cup (235 ml) of pasta water to loosen. Add the roasted cauliflower and the seedy bread crumb mixture. Toss well. Add a few tablespoons (60 ml) of vegetable broth or water to loosen it up a bit, if needed.

Add It!

Frozen peas are a great addition to this dish. Add 1 cup (130 g) of frozen peas to the strainer and drain your pasta right over the top. Add the pasta and peas together to the skillet.

Pesto Pasta with Roasted Grape Tomatoes and Asparagus

This pasta dish is bursting with fresh flavor, like summer in a bowl! The pesto is easily made in a food processor while the vegetables roast and the pasta boils. Throw it all together and you're eating dinner in no time!

16 ounces (455 g) penne (gluten-free, if desired)

1 bunch asparagus

2 pints (550 g) grape tomatoes, halved

1 tablespoon (15 ml) olive oil

½ teaspoon salt

1 recipe Mixed Greens Pepita Pesto (page 164)

1 cup (235 ml) reserved pasta water

1 tablespoon (15 ml) balsamic vinegar (optional)

Yield: 4 to 6 servings

Preheat the oven to 450°F (220°C, or gas mark 7). Line a rimmed baking sheet with parchment paper and set aside.

Cook the penne according to package directions, reserving 1 cup (235 ml) of the cooking water before draining.

Cut the woody ends off the asparagus and discard. Chop the asparagus spears into bite-size pieces. Place them on the prepared baking sheet with the cherry tomatoes, olive oil, and salt. Toss well to ensure all the vegetables are covered with the oil and salt. Bake for 10 to 15 minutes until they are tender and starting to brown.

Meanwhile, make the Mixed Greens Pepita Pesto if you haven't already.

Mix the Mixed Greens Pepita Pesto with the cooked penne and reserved cooking water. Add the roasted asparagus and tomatoes and toss. Add the balsamic vinegar, if using, and toss gently.

Add it!

Feel free to add fresh spinach or arugula for an extra dose of greens!

Kids in the Kitchen

Have your kids break off the woody stems of the asparagus and carefully slice the grape tomatoes in half using a serrated knife.

Rigatoni with Zucchini and Corn

This might be my husband's favorite recipe in the whole book. He couldn't stop eating it and said he could eat it every day. Considering how easy it is to make, he might just get his wish! This dish really shines in the summer with fresh from the farmers' market vegetables, but store-bought zucchini and frozen corn work just as well!

8 ounces (225 g) rigatoni or another medium-size pasta (gluten-free, if desired)

1 tablespoon (15 ml) olive oil

½ red onion, diced

3 cloves garlic, minced

1 large carrot, peeled and diced (about ½ cup [65 g] diced)

1 cup (164 g) fresh or frozen corn kernels

1 medium zucchini, diced

1 pint (275 g) grape tomatoes, halved

1 tablespoon (15 ml) tamari, coconut aminos, or soy sauce (gluten-free, if desired)

1 teaspoon dried basil

½ teaspoon salt, or to taste

¼ teaspoon black pepper, or to taste

1 tablespoon (15 ml) balsamic vinegar

Yield: 4 servings

Cook the rigatoni to al dente according to package directions. Reserve ¼ cup (60 ml) of the pasta cooking water before draining to use in the sauce, if needed.

Meanwhile, heat the olive oil in a large skillet over medium heat. Sauté the onion for 4 to 5 minutes until soft and translucent. Add the garlic and carrot and sauté for 4 to 5 minutes.

Add the corn, zucchini, tomatoes, tamari, basil, salt, and pepper. Sauté for 4 to 5 minutes until the tomatoes start to burst and let out their juices. Add the pasta to the skillet and toss well to mix. Add the reserved pasta water, if needed, to make it saucier. Stir in the balsamic vinegar and serve.

Add It!

Torn fresh basil added just before serving is wonderful in this dish.

Kids in the Kitchen

Kids as young as about four or five can use a vegetable peeler with supervision, so let them peel the carrots. Kids a bit older can use a small serrated knife to halve the tomatoes.

Rotini with Chunky Garden Veggie Marinara

I love making this sauce when our backyard garden is plentiful with ripe veggies. Feel free to use the vegetables you have available. Use summer squash instead of the zucchini, double up on the carrots and leave out the peppers, or swap the eggplant for meaty mushrooms. Make it your own!

12 ounces (340 g) rotini pasta or pasta of choice (gluten-free, if desired)

2 tablespoons (28 ml) olive oil

1 yellow onion, diced

2 cloves garlic, minced

1 small zucchini, diced

¾ cup peeled and diced eggplant (about ½ globe eggplant)

1 large carrot, peeled and diced

1 red bell pepper, seeded and diced

1 can (28 ounces, or 785 g) crushed tomatoes

1 teaspoon salt, or to taste

¼ teaspoon black pepper, or to taste

2 teaspoons dried basil

1 tablespoon (15 ml) balsamic vinegar

¼ cup (60 ml) low-sodium vegetable broth, plus more if needed

Yield: 6 servings

Cook the pasta according to package directions.

Heat the olive oil over medium heat in a large skillet. Add the onion and sauté for 5 to 6 minutes until soft and translucent. Add the garlic and sauté for 1 minute.

Add the zucchini, eggplant, carrot, and bell pepper and sauté for 7 to 8 minutes until the vegetables start to soften. Add a tablespoon or two (15 to 28 ml) of vegetable broth if the skillet gets dry.

Add the crushed tomatoes, salt, pepper, basil, balsamic vinegar, and ¼ cup (60 ml) of vegetable broth. Stir to combine. Simmer the sauce on low heat for 20 minutes, stirring occasionally.

Serve the sauce over the cooked noodles.

Pasta and Spinach
with Roasted Red Pepper Sauce

Are you trying to get your kids to branch out and try new veggies? This is a great place to start. Although it's made from roasted red red peppers, this sauce looks like the tomato-based marinara they're probably familiar with.

12 ounces (340 g) pasta of choice

1 tablespoon (15 ml) olive oil

½ sweet onion, diced

3 cloves garlic, minced

1 jar (16 ounces, or 455 g) roasted red peppers, drained well

2 tablespoons (32 g) tomato paste

1 tablespoon (15 ml) red wine vinegar

¾ cup (175 ml) unsweetened almond milk

1 tablespoon (8 g) cornstarch

1 tablespoon (16 g) mellow white miso paste (optional)

½ teaspoon salt, or to taste

2 cups (60 g) packed fresh baby spinach, chopped

Fresh chopped parsley, for garnish

Yield: 4 servings

Cook the pasta according to package directions. Drain and set aside.

Heat the olive oil in a small skillet over medium heat. Add the onion and sauté for 4 to 5 minutes until soft and translucent. Add the garlic and sauté for 1 minute.

In a high-speed blender, add the onion-garlic mixture, roasted red peppers, tomato paste, red wine vinegar, milk, cornstarch, miso (if using), and salt. Blend until smooth.

Pour the sauce into a large pot and bring to a boil. Simmer for 5 minutes or until thickened. Add the spinach and stir for 1 to 2 minutes until the spinach starts to wilt.

Add the pasta to the sauce and stir to combine. Sprinkle with parsley to garnish.

SERVING SUGGESTION: Chopped vegan sausages are a yummy addition to this pasta. We like the Field Roast brand. Slice them up and panfry them until crisp on the edges. Stir them into the pasta or serve them on the side.

Kids in the Kitchen

Have your kids blend the sauce. Make sure they have the lid on tight before starting the blender.

Pumpkin Maple-Glazed Penne
with Roasted Fall Vegetables

This pasta dish is fall in a bowl! While there is quite a bit of peeling and chopping involved, the final result is so worth it. You can find prechopped butternut squash in most stores these days, so feel free to take advantage of that time-saver if you wish. The subtle sweetness of the sauce pairs beautifully with the roasted vegetables. If you have picky eaters who won't eat some of these veggies, feel free to leave them out and double up on the ones they like.

FOR THE ROASTED FALL VEGETABLES:

1 cup (140 g) peeled and chopped butternut squash

1 cup (130 g) peeled and chopped carrots

1 cup (110 g) peeled and chopped parsnips

1 cup (88 g) halved Brussels sprouts

1 tablespoon (15 ml) olive oil

½ teaspoon dried thyme

½ teaspoon salt

⅛ teaspoon black pepper

FOR THE PASTA:

16 ounces (455 g) penne pasta (gluten-free, if desired)

½ cup (123 g) pure pumpkin purée (NOT pumpkin pie filling)

1 cup (235 ml) lite coconut milk

2 tablespoons (40 g) pure maple syrup

¾ teaspoon salt, or to taste

1 tablespoon (15 ml) olive oil (optional)

Yield: 5 servings

For the Roasted Fall Vegetables: Preheat the oven to 400°F (200°C, or gas mark 6). Line a baking sheet with parchment paper and set aside.

Toss the vegetables in a large bowl with the olive oil, thyme, salt, and pepper. Spread out onto the prepared baking sheet in an even layer. Roast for 15 minutes, stir, and roast for 10 to 15 more minutes until the vegetables are tender and browning on the sides.

For the Pasta: Meanwhile, cook the penne according to package directions. Be sure to salt your cooking water well.

When your pasta and vegetables have about 10 minutes cooking time left, whisk all the sauce ingredients in a large skillet over medium heat. Bring to a boil and then reduce the heat to low to simmer for 5 to 10 minutes until thickened a bit.

Add the cooked pasta and roasted vegetables to the skillet with the sauce and toss well to coat. Add the olive oil, if using. Season with extra salt and pepper, if desired.

NOTE: The pasta will continue to soak up the sauce when storing leftovers. You may need a splash of vegetable broth to loosen it up when reheating.

Kids in the Kitchen

Kids can help peel the carrots and parsnips, and they can halve the Brussels sprouts. They can also help whisk the sauce.

CHAPTER 7

One-Pot Wonders

The last thing anyone wants to do after enjoying a meal with their family is to stand in front of the sink washing numerous pots and pans. Enter these fabulous One-Pot Wonders! Bringing lots of flavor with very little fuss, these meals might just become staples in your home.

Easy Indian Lentils and Kidney Beans

Most Indian dishes contain a long list of spices, many of which you may not have in your pantry. This easy one-pot dish isn't exactly authentic, but it's flavorful and delicious. And it only requires one unique ingredient that you may not already have—garam masala. Garam masala is a spice blend consisting of many of the aromatic spices found in Indian cooking. It's a quick and easy way to get the flavors you crave with little to no fuss.

1½ tablespoons (21 g) coconut oil or (25 ml) olive oil

1 yellow onion, diced

3 cloves garlic, minced

2 teaspoons garam masala

½ teaspoon turmeric

2 tablespoons (32 g) tomato paste

1 can (15 ounces, or 425 g) diced tomatoes

¾ cup (144 g) dry brown lentils, picked over and rinsed well with cold water

1 can (15 ounces, or 425 g) red kidney beans, drained and rinsed (or 1½ cups [267 g] cooked beans)

1¼ cups (295 ml) low-sodium vegetable broth

1 tablespoon (9 g) coconut sugar or (15 g) brown sugar

1 teaspoon salt, or to taste

¼–½ cup (60–120 ml) lite coconut milk

Yield: 4 servings

Heat the coconut oil in a pot over medium heat. Add the onion and sauté for 5 to 6 minutes until softened and translucent. Add the garlic, garam masala, and turmeric and sauté for 1 minute until fragrant.

Add the tomato paste, tomatoes, lentils, kidney beans, and vegetable broth. Stir, increase the heat to high and bring to a boil, cover, and then reduce the heat to medium-low. Simmer for 30 to 35 minutes until the lentils are tender.

Add the coconut sugar and salt and stir well to incorporate. Add ¼ cup (60 ml) of lite coconut milk and stir. If the lentils seem thick and you prefer a looser dish, add another ¼ cup (60 ml) of lite coconut milk.

SERVING SUGGESTION: Serve with naan.

Italian Lentils and Rice

This dish doesn't seem like much at first glance, but it's pure comfort food in a bowl. Lentils and rice are a classic combination, and in this dish they're creamy, hearty, and filling.

2 tablespoons (28 ml) olive oil

1 yellow onion, diced

3 cloves garlic, minced

1 tablespoon (6 g) Italian seasoning

1 cup (192 g) dry green or brown lentils, picked over and rinsed well with cold water

4½ cups (1.1 L) low-sodium vegetable broth (may substitute half with water)

1 cup (185 g) jasmine rice, rinsed well in cold water (or quick-cook white or brown rice)

1 can (15 ounces, or 425 g) diced tomatoes, drained

2 tablespoons (28 ml) red wine vinegar

1 teaspoon salt, or to taste

¼ teaspoon black pepper, or to taste

3 tablespoons (12 g) nutritional yeast (optional)

2 handfuls of baby spinach (optional)

Yield: 4 to 6 servings

Heat the olive oil in a large, deep skillet over medium heat. Add the onion and sauté for 5 to 6 minutes until soft and translucent. Add the garlic and Italian seasoning and sauté for 1 minute. Add the lentils and vegetable broth and stir to combine. Increase the heat to high to bring to a boil, cover, and then reduce the heat to low and simmer for 25 minutes.

Stir in the rice, increase the heat to bring back to a boil, cover, and then reduce the heat to low and simmer for another 15 minutes until the lentils and rice are tender.

Add the drained tomatoes, red wine vinegar, salt, and pepper and stir. Add the nutritional yeast and baby spinach, if using, and stir to combine.

Spiced Chickpea Stew

Chunky, saucy, flavorful, and full of healthy plant-based protein, this stew couldn't be easier to make—and it's so darn yummy! Serve it with some crusty bread for soaking up every last bit of goodness in the bottom of your bowl.

2 tablespoons (28 ml) olive oil

1 yellow onion, diced

3 carrots, peeled and chopped

1½ teaspoons ground turmeric

1½ teaspoons chili powder

1 teaspoon cumin

½ teaspoon ground cinnamon

½ cup (120 ml) low-sodium vegetable broth

2 cans (15 ounces, or 425 g each) chickpeas, drained and rinsed (or 3 cups [492 g] cooked chickpeas)

1 can (15 ounces, or 425 g) diced tomatoes

1 teaspoon salt, or to taste

Fresh lime juice

Fresh chopped cilantro, for garnish (optional)

Yield: 4 servings

Heat the olive oil in a large skillet over medium heat. Add the onion and sauté until soft and translucent, about 5 to 6 minutes. Add the carrots, turmeric, chili powder, cumin, and cinnamon. Stir and sauté for 1 to 2 minutes.

Add the vegetable broth, chickpeas, tomatoes, and salt. Simmer for 15 minutes.

Take off the heat. Add a squeeze of lime juice and fresh cilantro, if using. Taste and adjust the seasoning, if necessary.

SERVING SUGGESTION: Serve with a hunk of crusty bread or over rice for an even heartier meal.

Kids in the Kitchen

Put your kids to work peeling carrots and rinsing the chickpeas. They can also portion out the spices in a little bowl.

Easy Thai Red Curry Noodles

This dish was a favorite among recipe testers. It's incredibly flavorful, so easy, and ready in under thirty minutes!

1 tablespoon (14 g) coconut oil or (15 ml) olive oil

1-inch (2.5 cm) knob ginger, peeled and minced

3 cloves garlic, minced

3 tablespoons (45 g) Thai red curry paste

1 tablespoon (16 g) natural creamy peanut butter

2 tablespoons (28 ml) tamari, coconut aminos, or soy sauce (gluten-free, if desired)

2 teaspoons coconut sugar or sweetener of choice

1 carrot, peeled and diced

1 red bell pepper, seeded and diced

4 cups (946 ml) low-sodium vegetable broth

8 ounces (225 g) thin rice noodles

2 cups (142 g) broccoli florets

1 can (15 ounces, or 440 ml) full-fat or lite coconut milk

Juice of 1 lime

Chopped cilantro, for garnish

Chopped peanuts, for garnish

Yield: 4 servings

Heat the coconut oil in a large deep skillet over medium heat. Add the ginger and garlic and sauté for 1 to 2 minutes to soften. Add the curry paste, peanut butter, tamari, and coconut sugar and stir until smooth. Add the carrot, bell pepper, and vegetable broth. Simmer for 8 to 10 minutes until tender.

Add the rice noodles to the skillet, stir, bring to a boil, and then reduce the heat to low. Simmer for 8 to 10 minutes until cooked through, stirring frequently to prevent sticking.

Add the broccoli, coconut milk, and lime juice. Cook for 1 to 2 minutes to heat through. Serve with the cilantro and chopped peanuts.

TIP: We like our broccoli to have a little crunch. If you like it softer, you can steam it for a few minutes before adding it to the noodles.

Quick Peanut Noodles

This easy dish is a kid favorite in our house. The creamy peanut sauce comes together easily with a whisk. Shredded carrots bulk up the noodles and provide added nutrition. Feel free to add any extra vegetables that your family enjoys. If you like extra saucy noodles, you may want to double the sauce.

12 ounces (340 g) udon or soba noodles

1 cup (110 g) shredded carrots

3 tablespoons (48 g) creamy peanut butter

2 tablespoons (28 ml) tamari, coconut aminos, or soy sauce (gluten-free, if desired)

2 tablespoons (28 ml) unseasoned rice vinegar

2 tablespoons (40 g) pure maple syrup

2 tablespoons (28 ml) sesame oil

3 scallions, sliced

¼ cup (36 g) chopped peanuts

Sriracha or crushed red pepper flakes (optional)

Yield: 4 to 6 servings

Cook the noodles according to package directions. Just before draining, add the carrots to the pot. Reserve 1 cup (235 ml) of cooking water and then drain the noodles and set aside.

Meanwhile, in a small bowl or measuring cup, whisk together the peanut butter, tamari, rice vinegar, maple syrup, and sesame oil.

Pour the sauce in the pot the noodles were cooked in. Then, pour the noodles and carrots back in the pot as well and stir well to combine. If you need to thin out the sauce, add the reserved noodle cooking water 1 tablespoon (15 ml) at a time until the desired consistency is reached.

Add the scallions and chopped peanuts and stir. Add a dash of sriracha or crushed red pepper flakes, if desired.

Swap It!

For a gluten-free options, use soba noodles, but be sure to read the package label as some brands do contain wheat.

Chili-Lime Quinoa
with Sweet Potatoes and Black Beans

This dish tastes almost like a super thick chili. The sweet potatoes balance the heat of the chili powder and the smokiness of the paprika perfectly. It's warm, creamy, and filling, with just a touch of crunch from crushed tortilla chips—comfort in a bowl!

1 tablespoon (15 ml) olive oil

½ yellow onion, diced

1 medium sweet potato, diced (about 3 cups [399 g])

1 tablespoon (8 g) chili powder

1 teaspoon smoked paprika

¾ cups (128 g) dry quinoa, rinsed well under cold water

1¾ cups (410 ml) low-sodium vegetable broth

1 can (15 ounces, or 425 g) black beans, drained and rinsed (or 1½ cups [258 g] cooked beans)

½ teaspoon salt, or to taste

¼ teaspoon black pepper, or to taste

Juice of 2 limes

Handful of fresh cilantro, chopped

Tortilla chips, for serving (see note)

Yield: 4 servings

Heat the olive oil in a large skillet over medium heat. Add the onion and sauté for 5 to 6 minutes until soft and translucent. Add the sweet potato, chili powder, and smoked paprika and sauté for 1 minute.

Add the quinoa and vegetable broth, increase the heat to high to bring to a boil, cover, and then reduce the heat to low. Simmer for 15 minutes until the quinoa is tender and has absorbed most of the liquid.

Add the black beans, salt, pepper, lime juice, and cilantro. Stir to combine.

Serve in individual bowls and crush some tortilla chips over the top.

Add it!

We love adding crushed tortilla chips to individual bowls just before serving for some crunch. You could also use whole tortilla chips to scoop up the mixture. Diced avocado would also be a great addition just before serving.

Broccoli, Green Bean, and Tofu Stir-Fry

This stir-fry is so fresh and crisp. There are no mushy veggies here! The sauce makes just enough to coat the veggies, but not drown them. Broccoli and green beans are two of the vegetables that my kids happily eat time and time again, but you can swap in zucchini or asparagus if desired. You could serve this stir-fry over rice, but sometimes, I like to step away from the grains for a moment and let the vegetables really shine on their own.

1 recipe Addictive Crispy Panfried Tofu (page 168)

¼ cup (60 ml) tamari, coconut aminos, or soy sauce (gluten-free, if desired)

¼ cup (60 ml) water

2 tablespoons (28 ml) rice vinegar

1 tablespoon (20 g) pure maple syrup

2 teaspoons sesame oil

1 tablespoon (15 ml) olive oil or peanut oil

½ red onion, sliced

4 cloves garlic, minced

2 tablespoons (12 g) chopped fresh ginger (Be sure to peel the ginger before you chop.)

1 tablespoon (8 g) cornstarch

1 head broccoli, chopped into bite-size florets

12 ounces (340 g) fresh green beans, halved

1 tablespoon (8 g) sesame seeds

Sriracha (optional)

Yield: 4 servings

Make the tofu as directed and set aside. There's no need to wash the pan since you'll use it again.

Whisk together the tamari, water, rice vinegar, maple syrup, and sesame oil in a small bowl. Set aside.

Using the same pan you used to make the tofu or another large pan, heat to medium heat and add the tablespoon (15 ml) of olive oil. Sauté the onion for 3 to 4 minutes until soft. Add the garlic and ginger and sauté for 1 to 2 minutes until fragrant. Add the cornstarch and stir well to coat.

Add the tamari mixture while whisking continuously until a smooth sauce is formed. Increase the heat to high and bring to a low bubble and then decrease the heat to medium-low. Add the broccoli and greens beans and cook for 1 to 2 minutes to heat through. Add the tofu back to the pan and stir to coat.

To finish, sprinkle with sesame seeds and add a dash of sriracha, if desired.

SERVING SUGGESTION: The sauce makes just enough to coat the tofu and veggies. If you choose to serve it with rice or noodles, you may want to double the sauce.

Swap It!

You may also make this recipe with Addictive Chewy Baked Tofu (page 168) instead of panfried, but, of course, then it wouldn't be a one-pot meal.

Sheet-Pan Tofu Fajitas

This recipe is high protein and very filling. Sometimes, I make it with just the portobello mushrooms or just the tofu, instead of both. And I often add sliced zucchini to the vegetables as well. Feel free to toss in whatever veggies you prefer.

1 package (14 ounces, or 390 g) extra-firm tofu, drained

2 portobello mushroom caps, stem and gills removed, sliced

3 bell peppers, a variety of colors, seeded and sliced

1 red onion, halved and sliced

¼ cup (60 ml) grapeseed oil or other high heat neutral oil

¼ cup (60 ml) vegan Worcestershire sauce

¼ cup (60 ml) fresh lime juice

1 tablespoon (8 g) chili powder

2 teaspoons cumin

1 teaspoon garlic powder

1 teaspoon onion powder

1 teaspoon dried oregano

1 teaspoon smoked paprika

½ teaspoon salt, or to taste

¼ teaspoon black pepper, or to taste

1 recipe BEST Guacamole (page 162) or store-bought guacamole

1 recipe Creamy Cumin Ranch Dressing (page 162; optional)

Tortillas, for serving (corn tortillas for gluten-free)

Yield: 6 servings

Preheat the oven to 400°F (200°C, or gas mark 6). Line 2 baking sheets with parchment paper and set aside.

Cut the tofu into long thin strips about the same size as the bell peppers and mushrooms.

In a large bowl, whisk together the grapeseed oil, Worcestershire sauce, lime juice, chili powder, cumin, garlic powder, onion powder, oregano, smoked paprika, salt, and pepper.

Add the bell peppers and onion and stir well to coat. Using kitchen tongs, remove the peppers and onions, shaking off any excess marinade, and transfer to one of the prepared baking sheets in an even layer.

Add the mushrooms and tofu to the remaining marinade and stir well to coat. Transfer them, shaking off any excess marinade, to the other prepared baking sheet.

Bake both pans for 20 minutes, stir the peppers and onions, and flip over the tofu and mushroom slices. Bake for another 10 to 15 minutes until the vegetables are tender and the edges are browned.

To serve, spread a dollop of BEST Guacamole on the center of a tortilla, top with a few slices of tofu, and few slices of mushrooms, and several slices of bell peppers and onions. Drizzle with the Creamy Cumin Ranch Dressing, if using. Repeat with the remaining ingredients.

OPTIONAL: Press the tofu for 20 minutes before cutting it into strips. I find pressing extra-firm or super-firm tofu doesn't make much of a difference unless it seems very wet when it comes out of the package. If you choose to press your tofu, wrap the block of tofu in several paper towels or a clean kitchen towel and place on a plate. Place another plate on top of the tofu and weigh down the top plate. Cans or bags of beans or rice work well for this or a heavy skillet. This tower may start to topple as the tofu loses liquid, so don't use anything breakable, like glass jars, as a weight.

NOTE: Be sure to check the label on the Worcestershire sauce if you need gluten-free. The Wizard's brand is vegan and gluten-free.

Summer Vegetable Tomato Rice Skillet

This dish has all the wonderful flavors and textures of Ratatouille, a French vegetable stew. Here, I'm pairing it with fragrant Jasmine rice and a touch of miso paste for umami and it's all done in one pot!

2 tablespoons (28 ml) olive oil

1 yellow onion, diced

2 cloves garlic, diced

1 zucchini, diced

1 globe eggplant, peeled and diced

1 large carrot, peeled and diced

1 sweet bell pepper, any color, seeded and diced

1 tablespoon (16 g) mellow white miso paste (optional)

1 cup (185 g) jasmine rice or quick-cook rice

2 cans (15 ounces, or 425 g each) tomato sauce

2 cups (475 ml) low-sodium vegetable broth

1 teaspoon salt, or to taste

¼ teaspoon black pepper, or to taste

2 teaspoons dried basil

Pinch of crushed red pepper flakes (optional)

Yield: 4 servings

Heat the olive oil in a large deep skillet over medium heat. Add the onion and sauté for 5 to 6 minutes until soft and translucent. Add the garlic, zucchini, eggplant, carrot, and bell pepper. Sauté for 4 to 5 minutes until starting to soften and reduce.

Add the miso paste, if using, and stir to blend. Add the rice and stir to combine.

Add the tomato sauce, vegetable broth, salt, pepper, and basil and stir well to combine. Increase the heat to high to bring to a boil, cover, and then reduce the heat to low and simmer for 15 minutes, stirring occasionally to prevent sticking, until the rice is tender.

Add the crushed red pepper flakes, if using, and stir.

Add it!

For additional protein, feel free to add a 15-ounce (425 g) can of chickpeas, drained and rinsed, when adding the diced vegetables. Or, you can stir in 1 cup (130 g) of frozen green peas at the end.

Kids in the Kitchen

Kids can help chop the vegetables and stir the rice during cooking so it doesn't stick.

Skillet Chickpea Chilaquiles

I am a huge chips and salsa addict, and this dish is kind of like eating nachos for dinner, so I could pretty much eat this every day. Crispy tortilla chips in a bath of saucy southwest flavors—it's like my dream come true! I eat these chilaquiles with a knife and fork, but my kids like to get right in there with their hands and get messy. Whatever floats your boat!

FOR THE CHILAQUILES:

1 can (15 ounces, or 425 g) chickpeas, rinsed and drained (or 1½ cups [246 g] cooked chickpeas)

2 tablespoons (28 ml) olive oil

1 yellow onion, diced

2 cloves garlic, minced

1½ tablespoons (12 g) chili powder

2 teaspoons cumin

2 teaspoons dried oregano

1 cup (164 g) fresh or frozen corn kernels

1 can (28 ounces, or 785 g) crushed tomatoes

1½ teaspoons salt, or to taste

8 ounces (225 g) unsalted corn tortillas chips (about 8 cups [208 g])

FOR SERVING:

BEST Guacamole (page 162) or store-bought guacamole, or avocado slices

Creamy Cumin Ranch Dressing (page 162) or store-bought southwest ranch dressing

Thinly sliced radishes

Diced white or red onion

Chopped fresh cilantro

Yield: 4 servings

For the Chilaquiles: Pour the rinsed and drained chickpeas out on a cutting board and chop them up a bit. Alternatively, you can add them to a food processor and pulse a few times. Set aside.

Heat the olive oil in a large, deep skillet over medium heat. Add the onion and sauté for 5 to 6 minutes until soft and translucent. Add the garlic, chili powder, cumin, and oregano and sauté for 1 minute until the spices are fragrant. Add the chickpeas, corn, crushed tomatoes, and salt and simmer for about 10 minutes until hot.

Add the tortilla chips to the skillet and gently stir to coat.

Serve immediately with your toppings of choice.

NOTE: If you aren't going to eat the whole recipe at once, keep the tortilla chips separate. Add one portion of chips to a bowl, then pour on some of the sauce, and garnish with desired toppings.

TIP: Serve immediately for crispy chips. If you like the chips softer, wait 5 to 10 minutes for the tortillas chips to soak up the sauce.

Kidney Bean Chili

This is a delicious, flavorful chili reminiscent of traditional versions, but packed with healthy plant protein. Made with all pantry ingredients and ready in under thirty minutes, this is one of my go-to dishes— especially in the fall and winter when a big mug of chili warms us right up! Garnish it with your choice of toppings.

FOR THE CHILI:

1 tablespoon (15 ml) olive oil

1 yellow onion, diced

1 green bell pepper, seeded and diced

3 carrots, peeled and shredded

2 cloves garlic, minced

¼ cup (64 g) tomato paste

2 tablespoons (16 g) chili powder

1 tablespoon (7 g) cumin

2 cans (15 ounces, or 425 g each) kidney beans, drained and rinsed (or 3 cups [531 g] cooked beans)

2 cans (15 ounces, or 425 g each) diced tomatoes

1 can (15 ounces, or 425 g) tomato sauce

1½ teaspoons salt, or to taste

TOPPINGS (OPTIONAL):

Dairy-free sour cream

Sliced scallions

Diced Avocado

Chopped cilantro

Yield: 4 servings

Heat the olive oil in a large soup pot over medium-high heat. Add the onion and sauté for 5 to 6 minutes until soft and translucent. Add the bell pepper, carrots, and garlic and sauté for 4 to 5 minutes until starting to soften. Add the tomato paste, chili powder, and cumin and stir until smooth.

Add the remaining ingredients and stir. Increase the heat to bring to a boil and then reduce to medium-low heat and simmer for 10 to 15 minutes.

Taste and adjust the seasoning, if needed. Serve with your toppings of choice.

Kids in the Kitchen

Kids can help drain and rinse the beans and portion out the spices. Older kids can help chop the vegetables.

CHAPTER 8

Comforting Casseroles

Casseroles are like a big hug. They're warm, inviting, and comforting. Once everything is in the baking dish, all you must do is wait patiently for it to get hot and bubbly in the oven. Use this time to help the kids with their homework, respond to emails, or pop open a bottle of wine!

Potpie Noodle Casserole

This is just like potpie, but without the fuss of a pie crust. Bonus: there are noodles in this casserole that you don't get in traditional potpie. My kids and husband went crazy for this dish, as did everyone who tested it.

FOR THE POTPIE NOODLES:

8 ounces (225 g) rotini or other medium shape pasta, such as rigatoni (gluten-free, if desired)

2 tablespoons (28 ml) olive oil

1 yellow onion, diced

2 ribs celery, diced

2 tablespoons (16 g) all-purpose flour (see note)

1 tablespoon (6 g) Italian seasoning

3 tablespoons (45 ml) tamari, coconut aminos, or soy sauce (gluten-free, if desired)

¼ teaspoon salt, or to taste

¼ teaspoon black pepper, or to taste

2 cups (475 ml) low-sodium vegetable broth

1 package (16 ounces, or 455 g) frozen mixed vegetables (corn, peas, carrots, and green beans)

1 cup (235 ml) cashew milk or other creamy plant-based milk (such as lite coconut or unsweetened soy)

2 tablespoons (8 g) nutritional yeast (optional)

Preheat the oven to 350°F (180°C, or gas mark 4).

For the Potpie Noodles: Cook the rotini to al dente, according to package directions. Drain and set aside.

Meanwhile, heat the olive oil over medium heat in a large, deep skillet. Add the onion and celery. Sauté for 5 to 6 minutes until softened and the onion is translucent. Add the flour and stir until combined and no flour is visible. Add the Italian seasoning, tamari, salt, and pepper and stir to combine.

Slowly pour in the vegetable broth, whisking continuously to ensure a smooth sauce. Add the mixed vegetables, cashew milk, and nutritional yeast, if using. Stir to combine, bring to a simmer, and cook for a few minutes to thicken. Add the cooked rotini and stir again to combine. Transfer the mixture to a 9- × 13-inch (23 × 33 cm) baking dish.

Swap It!

Use brown rice flour or a gluten-free flour blend instead of all-purpose flour for a gluten-free option.

Add it!

Feel free to add a 15-ounce (425 g) can of drained and rinsed chickpeas for added protein.

FOR THE GARLIC BREAD CRUMBS:

¼ cup (13 g) panko bread crumbs or regular bread crumbs (gluten-free, if desired)

¼ cup (15 g) nutritional yeast or more bread crumbs

1 teaspoon granulated garlic powder

1 tablespoon (14 g) melted plant-based butter or coconut oil

Yield: 4 to 6 servings

For the Garlic Bread Crumbs: In a small bowl, stir together the panko bread crumbs, nutritional yeast, and garlic powder. Pour the melted butter over the bread crumbs mixture while stirring to moisten thoroughly.

Sprinkle the Garlic Bread Crumbs over the top of the casserole. Bake for 20 to 25 minutes until the bread crumbs are toasted and the sauce is thick and bubbly.

Kids in the Kitchen

Let the kids sprinkle the Garlic Bread Crumbs on the casserole before baking.

Baked Garlic White Mac and Cheese
with Garlic Bread Crumb Topping

All credit for the inspiration for this dish goes to my son. He came up with the idea for garlic mac and cheese, and I took it from there. This dish is super creamy and tastes indulgent. No one will ever know there's cauliflower in there! If you want a milder garlic flavor, you can leave out the garlic powder in the bread crumbs.

FOR THE GARLIC WHITE MAC AND CHEESE:

16 ounces (455 g) large elbow noodles or medium shells

1 head cauliflower, cut into florets (about 5–6 cups [600–700 g])

2 cloves garlic, peeled

1½ cups (355 ml) unsweetened plain almond or cashew milk, or milk of choice

3 tablespoons (48 g) mellow white miso paste

1 teaspoon salt, or to taste

¼ teaspoon black pepper (optional)

Preheat the oven to 350°F (180°C, or gas mark 4). Lightly spray a 9- × 13-inch (23 × 33 cm) baking dish with cooking spray and set aside.

For the Garlic White Mac and Cheese: Cook the noodles according to package directions.

Meanwhile, place the cauliflower and garlic in a large pot and cover with water. Bring to a boil over high heat and then reduce the heat to medium-low. Simmer for 7 to 8 minutes until the cauliflower is tender and easily pierced with a knife. Drain.

Place the drained cauliflower and garlic into a high-speed blender along with the milk, miso, salt, and pepper, if using. Blend until smooth.

Once the noodles are done, pour the sauce over the noodles and stir to coat well. Pour the mixture in the prepared baking dish.

Kids in the Kitchen

With your supervision, have the kids carefully pour the ingredients in the blender and press the buttons to blend. They can also sprinkle the bread crumbs on the casserole before you put it in the oven.

FOR THE GARLIC BREAD CRUMB TOPPING:

¼ cup (13 g) panko bread crumbs (gluten-free, if desired)

¼ cup (15 g) nutritional yeast or more bread crumbs

1 teaspoon garlic powder

1 tablespoon (15 ml) melted plant-based butter or coconut oil

Yield: 6 servings

For the Garlic Bread Crumb Topping: In a small bowl, combine the panko bread crumbs, nutritional yeast, and garlic powder. Drizzle in the melted butter while stirring. Stir well to ensure the entire mixture is moistened. Sprinkle evenly over the noodles in the baking dish.

Bake for 20 to 25 minutes until the sauce is bubbly and the bread crumbs are lightly golden brown.

SERVING SUGGESTION: If you're short on time or simply don't want to dirty another dish, serve this up straight from the pan without the bread crumbs. It's seriously so good!

Spinach and Artichoke Stuffed Shells

A super creamy spinach and artichoke filling stuffed inside tender pasta shells and smothered in the perfect marinara sauce—it's heaven on a plate!

1 package (14 ounces, or 390 g) extra-firm tofu, drained

12 ounces (340 g) jumbo pasta shells (gluten-free, if desired)

2 tablespoons (28 ml) olive oil

1 yellow onion, diced

3 cloves garlic, minced

2 teaspoons dried basil

½ teaspoon salt, or to taste

¼ teaspoon black pepper, or to taste

Pinch of ground nutmeg

½ cup (60 ml) unsweetened plain almond milk or milk of choice

1 tablespoon (16 g) miso paste (optional)

2 packed cups (about 60 g) fresh spinach

1 can (14 ounces, or 390 g) artichoke hearts, drained and rinsed

1 recipe Quick and Easy Marinara Sauce (page 165) or store-bought marinara sauce

Yield: 4 to 6 servings

Preheat the oven to 350°F (180°C, or gas mark 4).

To press the tofu, wrap the block of tofu in several paper towels or a clean kitchen towel and place on a plate. Place another plate on top of the tofu and weigh down the top plate. Cans or bags of beans or rice work well for this or a heavy skillet. This tower may start to topple as the tofu loses liquid, so don't use anything breakable, like glass jars, as a weight. Press for 20 minutes and then unwrap and cut the block in half.

Meanwhile, cook the pasta shells according to package directions. Cook them until just al dente as they will continue to cook in the oven once filled. If you overcook, they will be harder to handle when filling.

Meanwhile, heat the olive oil over medium heat in a small skillet. Add the onion and sauté for 5 to 6 minutes until soft and translucent. Add the garlic and sauté for 1 minute.

In the bowl of a food processor, place ½ block of the pressed tofu, the cooked onions and garlic, basil, salt, pepper, nutmeg, almond milk, and miso paste, if using. Purée. Transfer to a mixing bowl and set aside.

In the same food processor bowl (no need to wipe it out), add the spinach, artichoke hearts, and remaining ½ block of tofu. Pulse several times, scraping down the sides as needed, until chopped but not puréed. You want this mixture to have a bit of texture. Transfer to the mixing bowl with the purée and mix well until combined.

Add 2 cups (475 ml) of Quick and Easy Marinara Sauce to the bottom of a 9- × 13-inch (23 × 33 cm) baking dish. Take one jumbo pasta shell and fill it with 1 to 2 tablespoons of spinach artichoke mixture. Place on top of the Quick and Easy Marinara Sauce. Repeat with the remaining shells.

Bake for 25 to 30 minutes until hot. Serve with extra Quick and Easy Marinara Sauce, if desired.

NOTE: You need about 25 to 30 pasta shells for this recipe, so you likely won't use all the pasta shells from the package. I recommend making more than you will need, however, as shells sometimes tend to break when cooked and you won't be able to use those.

Sloppy Joe Casserole
with Cornbread Crust

This is one of those down-home comfort food meals that make you feel all warm and cozy inside. Saucy, sloppy beans and veggies are covered in a hearty cornbread crust. You'll want to lick your plate clean.

FOR THE CASSEROLE:

2 tablespoons (28 ml) olive oil

½ red onion, diced

2 cloves garlic, minced

2 carrots, peeled and diced

1 green bell pepper, seeded and diced

1 can (15 ounces, or 425 g) red kidney beans, drained and rinsed

1 can (15 ounces, or 425 g) cannellini beans (white kidney beans), drained and rinsed

1 can (15 ounces, or 425 g) tomato sauce

¼ cup (60 g) ketchup

¼ cup (60 g) organic brown sugar

2 tablespoons (28 ml) vegan Worcestershire sauce

1 teaspoon yellow mustard

1 teaspoon dried oregano

2 teaspoons liquid smoke (optional)

½ teaspoon salt, or to taste

¼ teaspoon black pepper, or to taste

1 cup (164 g) fresh or frozen corn kernels

FOR THE CORNBREAD CRUST:

1¼ cups (175 g) cornmeal

¾ cup (94 g) white whole wheat flour

1 teaspoon baking powder

½ teaspoon salt

1¼ cup (285 ml) unsweetened plain almond milk or milk of choice

½ cup (160 g) pure maple syrup

¼ cup (60 ml) vegetable oil

Yield: 6 servings

Preheat the oven to 400°F (200°C, or gas mark 6).

For the Casserole: Heat the olive oil in a large skillet over medium heat. Add the onion and sauté for 5 to 6 minutes until soft and translucent. Add the garlic, carrots, and bell pepper and sauté for 4 to 5 minutes until starting to soften. Add the remaining ingredients, except the corn, and stir well. Simmer for 10 to 15 minutes, stirring occasionally, until thick and bubbly. Add the corn and stir to combine.

For the Cornbread Crust: Meanwhile, whisk the cornmeal, flour, baking powder, and salt in a mixing bowl. Whisk the almond milk, maple syrup, and vegetable oil in a separate mixing bowl. Pour the dry ingredients into the wet ingredients and stir well to combine.

Pour the sloppy joe mixture into an 8- × 11-inch (20 × 28 cm) or similar casserole dish. Pour the cornbread mix over the top and gently smooth out in an even layer. Be careful not to push the cornbread mix into the sloppy joe mixture, although it's okay if a little bit seeps through.

Bake for 25 to 28 minutes until a toothpick inserted in the cornbread comes out clean. Let rest for 10 minutes before serving.

Kids in the Kitchen
Kids can whisk the cornbread together.

Vegetarian Lentil Cottage Pie

This is not your typical shepherd's pie! Made with lentils, butternut squash, cauliflower, and spices in a rich savory tomato sauce and topped off with creamy carrot mashed potatoes, this is comfort food at its best!

FOR THE FILLING:

1½ cups (210 g) peeled and diced butternut squash

1½ cups (150 g) cauliflower florets

2 tablespoons (28 ml) olive oil

1 onion, diced

2 cloves garlic, minced

3 tablespoons (48 g) tomato paste

2 tablespoons (28 ml) vegan Worcestershire sauce

2 tablespoons (28 ml) tamari, coconut aminos, or soy sauce

1½ teaspoons dried thyme

1 teaspoon salt, or to taste

¼ teaspoon black pepper, or to taste

1½ cups (355 ml) low-sodium vegetable broth, plus more as needed

2 cups (396 g) cooked brown or green lentils

FOR THE MASH:

4 cups (440 g) diced and peeled potatoes (preferably Yukon Gold)

2 carrots, peeled and diced

2 cloves garlic, minced

1 tablespoon (15 ml) olive oil

1 teaspoon salt, or to taste

Unsweetened plant-based milk to thin, if needed

Yield: 6 servings

Preheat the oven to 400°F (200°C, or gas mark 6). Lightly spray a 2½-quart (2.4 L) casserole dish with cooking spray and set aside.

Place the butternut squash and cauliflower in a pot and add enough water to cover the vegetables. Cover, bring to a boil, reduce the heat, and simmer for about 15 to 20 minutes until tender, but not mushy. Drain.

For the Mash: Meanwhile, place the potatoes and carrots in a pot with enough to cover them. Cover, bring to a boil, and then reduce the heat and simmer for 15 to 20 minutes until the vegetables are very soft. Drain and return to the pot. Add the garlic, olive oil, and salt. Using a potato masher, mash the vegetables until smooth; the carrots may not get as smooth as the potatoes and that's okay, just mash them as best you can. Add a splash or two of milk to thin, if needed.

For the Filling: In a large skillet on the stove, heat 2 tablespoons (28 ml) olive oil over medium heat. Add the onion and sauté until translucent, about 5 to 6 minutes. Add the garlic and sauté for 1 minute. Add the tomato paste, Worcestershire sauce, tamari, thyme, salt, and pepper. Stir to combine and cook for another 2 to 3 minutes.

Add the vegetable broth, lentils, and squash-cauliflower mixture and stir to combine. Simmer for 5 to 10 minutes until the mixture is thick but saucy. If this mixture seems too thick, add another ¼ to ½ cup (60 to 120 ml) of vegetable broth to loosen it up.

Pour the lentil filling in the casserole dish and spread evenly. Spoon the mashed potato mixture over the top and spread until even. Be careful not to press down too hard or the potatoes will end up in the filling instead of on top of it. Alternatively, you could let the filling cool first before adding the potatoes to the top. Bake for 20 minutes until hot and bubbly.

Kids in the Kitchen

Older kids can help peel and chop vegetables. Kids of all ages can help break the cauliflower into florets and mash the potatoes and carrots once cooked.

Black Bean and Zucchini Enchiladas

These enchiladas are always a hit! They are so easy to make, but they taste like total comfort food. The sauce is an easy, nontraditional blend of white beans and salsa, bringing even more plant-based protein to the party. You will not miss the cheese, I promise!

1 tablespoon (15 ml) olive oil

½ red onion, diced

2 cloves garlic, minced

1 red bell pepper, seeded and diced

½ zucchini, diced (about 1 cup [120 g])

2 teaspoons cumin, divided

½ teaspoon salt, divided, or to taste

1 can (15 ounces, or 425 g) black beans, rinsed and drained (or 1½ cups [258 g] cooked beans)

1 jar (16 ounces, or 455 g) tomato-based salsa

1 can (15 ounces, or 425 g) cannellini beans (white kidney beans), rinsed and drained (or 1½ cups [267 g] cooked beans)

½ teaspoon chili powder

½ cup (120 ml) water or low-sodium vegetable broth

8 corn or flour tortillas (corn tortillas for gluten-free)

TOPPINGS OF CHOICE (OPTIONAL):

BEST Guacamole (page 162)

Creamy Cumin Ranch Dressing (page 162)

Sliced jalapeños

Cilantro

Diced tomatoes

Yield: 4 servings

Preheat the oven to 350°F (180°C, or gas mark 4).

Heat the olive oil in a skillet over medium heat. Sauté the onion until translucent, about 5 to 6 minutes. Add the garlic, bell pepper, zucchini, 1 teaspoon of cumin, and ¼ teaspoon of salt and sauté for 2 minutes. Add the black beans and stir to combine. Turn the heat to low to keep warm while you make the sauce.

Combine the salsa, white beans, 1 teaspoon of cumin, chili powder, water, and ¼ teaspoon of salt in a blender or food processor. Purée until smooth.

Add 1 cup (235 ml) of the sauce to the black bean–zucchini mixture and stir to combine.

Pour ½ cup (120 ml) of the sauce in the bottom of a 7- × 11-inch (18 × 28 cm) baking dish.

Place about ⅓ cup (90 g) of filling in one tortilla, roll up, and place seam-side down in the baking dish. Repeat with the remaining tortillas.

Top the enchiladas with the remaining sauce and any remaining filling. Bake for 20 minutes. Garnish with your toppings of choice.

TIP: Slightly warming the tortillas will make them more pliable for folding.

Add It!
Add 1 cup (164 g) of corn kernels to the filling, if desired.

Kids in the Kitchen
Have your kids make the sauce and assemble the enchiladas.

Tortilla Enchilada Casserole

This is another one of my favorite recipes in this book. I love the combination of the savory, smoky enchilada sauce and subtly sweet dressing. It's loaded with healthy veggies and filling beans. And the kids love it, too!

FOR THE ENCHILADA SAUCE:

1 can (15 ounces, or 425 g) tomato sauce

½ cup (120 ml) low-sodium vegetable broth

2 tablespoons (16 g) chili powder

1 teaspoon cumin

1½ teaspoons smoked paprika

½ teaspoon salt, or to taste

½ teaspoon onion powder

¼ teaspoon dried oregano

Pinch of cayenne (optional) for extra heat

FOR THE CASSEROLE:

2 tablespoons (28 ml) olive oil

1 yellow onion, diced

2 cloves garlic, minced

1 zucchini, diced

1 red bell pepper, seeded and diced

1 orange or yellow pepper, seeded and diced (or another red bell pepper)

1 cup (164 g) fresh or frozen corn kernels

1 teaspoon cumin

½ teaspoon oregano

½ teaspoon salt, or to taste

¼ teaspoon black pepper, or to taste

1 can (15 ounces, or 425 g) black beans, rinsed and drained

4 flour tortillas (8 inches, or 20 cm each) or 6 corn tortillas (6 inches, or 15 cm each) for gluten-free, cut in half

1 recipe Creamy Cumin Ranch Dressing (page 162)

Yield: 6 servings

Preheat the oven to 350°F (180°C, or gas mark 4).

For the Enchilada Sauce: Combine all the ingredients in small pot over medium-high heat. When it starts to bubble, reduce the heat to low and simmer for 10 to 15 minutes. Set aside.

For the Casserole: Meanwhile, heat the olive oil in a large skillet over medium heat. Add the onion and sauté for 5 to 6 minutes until softened and translucent. Add the garlic, zucchini, bell peppers, corn, cumin, oregano, salt, and pepper and sauté for 5 to 6 minutes until softened.

Pour ¼ cup (60 ml) of the Enchilada Sauce in the bottom of an 8- × 8-inch (20 × 20 cm) baking dish. Lay 4 pieces of tortilla on the sauce, flat side against the sides of the baking dish. Use 6 pieces if you're using corn tortillas; get creative and fill the spaces to cover the bottom of the dish. The curved sides will overlap each other a bit. Spread half of the vegetable mixture on top, followed by half of the black beans.

Repeat the process, laying the other 4 pieces of tortillas on top of the beans like before, followed by ¼ cup (60 ml) of Enchilada Sauce, the remaining vegetables, and the remaining beans. Dollop ½ cup (120 ml) of the Creamy Cumin Ranch Dressing over the top and carefully spread it out with a spatula.

Place the baking dish on a cookie sheet to prevent spills and bake for 20 minutes until hot.

Kids in the Kitchen

Kids can cut the tortillas and help assemble the casserole.

Pesto Lasagna

My family can't get enough of this lasagna! The pesto is so flavorful and magically imparts a "cheesy" flavor. I promise you that omnivores and carnivores alike will love this recipe.

1 package (14 ounces, or 390 g) firm or extra-firm tofu, drained

1 recipe Quick and Easy Marinara Sauce (page 165)

1 recipe Mixed Greens Pepita Pesto (page 164)

1 tablespoon (15 ml) apple cider vinegar

½ teaspoon salt, or to taste

9–10 oven-ready lasagna noodles (gluten-free, if desired)

½ cup (25 g) panko bread crumbs (gluten-free, if desired)

½ teaspoon garlic powder

½ teaspoon dried oregano

1 tablespoon (15 ml) melted plant-based butter or coconut oil

Yield: 6 servings

Preheat the oven to 350°F (180°C, or gas mark 4).

Press the tofu for 20 minutes. Wrap the block of tofu in several paper towels or a clean kitchen towel and place on a plate. Place another plate on top of the tofu and weigh down the top plate. Cans or bags of beans or rice work well for this or a heavy skillet. This tower may start to topple as the tofu loses liquid, so don't use anything breakable, like glass jars, as a weight.

Meanwhile, make the Quick and Easy Marinara Sauce and set aside.

While the sauce is simmering, make the Mixed Greens Pepita Pesto, adding the additional 1 tablespoon (15 ml) of apple cider vinegar and ½ teaspoon of salt.

In a food processor, combine the pressed tofu and the prepared pesto. Process until combined well.

In an 8- × 11-inch (20 × 28 cm) casserole dish, ladle 1 cup (235 ml) of Quick and Easy Marinara Sauce in the bottom. On top, place 3 lasagna noodles, trying not to overlap, although a slight overlap is fine. Break off pieces of a fourth noodle to fill in any remaining spaces on the sides. Dollop 1½ cups (390 g) of the pesto mixture on top of the first layer of noodles and gently spread it out to cover all the noodles. Pour 1 cup (235 ml) of the Quick and Easy Marinara Sauce on top of the pesto and gently spread it out evenly. Repeat with 3 more noodles, the rest of the pesto mixture, and another 1 cup (235 ml) of Quick and Easy Marinara Sauce. Finish with the final 3 noodles, again breaking up an extra one to fill in any spaces, if necessary, and follow with 1 more cup (235 ml) of the Quick and Easy Marinara Sauce.

Kids in the Kitchen

Kids can make the Mixed Greens Pepita Pesto, help assemble the casserole, and prepare the bread crumb topping.

Cover the casserole dish with aluminum foil and bake for 30 minutes.

Meanwhile, in a small bowl, combine the panko bread crumbs, garlic powder, and oregano. Mix well. Pour the melted butter over the bread crumbs while stirring to thoroughly moisten all of them.

After 30 minutes of baking, uncover the lasagna and evenly sprinkle on the bread crumbs. Bake for another 8 to 10 minutes until the bread crumbs are toasted and golden brown.

Cut into squares and serve with the remaining Quick and Easy Marinara Sauce.

CHAPTER 9

Center Stage Vegetables

Vegetables make great side dishes, but there is no need to continually relegate them to that position. Vegetables can be hearty, filling, and appealing as the star of the plate. The following main dishes are some you can really sink your teeth into, and you won't miss the meat!

Cauliflower Steaks
with Lentils and Romesco Sauce

We eat a lot of cauliflower in this house. It's such a versatile vegetable that can take on nearly any role. It can even be the star of the plate! Perfectly roasted, thick cauliflower slices on a bed of protein-packed, herby lentils and smoky Romesco Sauce—it's a restaurant-worthy dinner!

FOR THE CAULIFLOWER STEAKS:

2 heads cauliflower

2 tablespoons (28 ml) olive oil

¼ teaspoon salt, or to taste

¼ teaspoon black pepper, or to taste

¼ teaspoon garlic powder

FOR THE LENTILS:

1 cup (192 g) dry French green lentils or brown lentils, picked over and rinsed well with cold water

3 cups (700 ml) low-sodium vegetable broth or water

1 teaspoon dried thyme

¼ teaspoon salt, or to taste

⅛ teaspoon black pepper, or to taste

1 tablespoon (15 ml) fresh lemon juice

2 tablespoons (8 g) chopped fresh parsley

FOR SERVING:

1 recipe Romesco Sauce (page 166)

Finely chopped almonds, for garnish

Yield: 4 servings

For the Cauliflower Steaks: Preheat the oven to 400°F (200°C, or gas mark 6).

Place a head of cauliflower stem-side up on a cutting board. Cut it in half through the middle of the stem. Carefully trim away all the green leaves from both halves, taking care not to cut the florets from the core. If the stem is rather long, cut the bottom half off, again being very careful not to cut too far up so the florets stay attached. Now, place one half stem-side down and cut a 1-inch (2.5 cm) slice off the middle. This is your "steak." Repeat with the other half and then repeat the whole process with the other head of cauliflower. Save the remaining florets that you aren't using for steaks for another time.

Brush both sides of each "steak" generously with the olive oil. In a small bowl, stir together the salt, pepper, and garlic powder. Sprinkle on the cauliflower steaks; you likely won't use it all. Roast the cauliflower for 15 minutes, gently flip over, and roast for 10 more minutes until golden brown on both sides.

For the Lentils: Meanwhile, place the lentils, vegetable broth, and thyme in a pot on the stove. Bring to a boil, cover, and reduce the heat to low. Simmer for 20 minutes or until tender. Drain and return the lentils to the pot. Add the salt, pepper, lemon juice, and parsley. Stir, taste, and adjust the seasoning, if necessary.

To serve: Ladle ¼ to ½ cup (60 to 120 ml) of Romesco Sauce on each plate, topped with one-quarter of the lentils and one cauliflower steak. Garnish with the chopped almonds.

Crispy Breaded Eggplant
with Spaghetti and Marinara

This crispy breaded eggplant is so good even on its own. Sometimes, I make it just for snacking. To make it a meal, I've paired it with spaghetti and marinara, a classic combo that usually involves cheese, but with all the flavor here, you just don't need it!

1 large eggplant, peeled and sliced into ¼-inch (6 mm) rounds

½ cup (63 g) all-purpose flour (or a gluten-free flour blend, if desired)

½ teaspoon salt, divided

¼ teaspoon black pepper

½ cup (120 ml) lite coconut milk

1¼ cups (63 g) panko bread crumbs (or gluten-free bread crumbs)

¼ cup (15 g) nutritional yeast or more bread crumbs

½ teaspoon garlic powder

2 teaspoons Italian seasoning

1 teaspoon dried oregano

8 ounces (225 g) spaghetti noodles (gluten-free, if desired)

1 recipe Quick and Easy Marinara Sauce (page 165)

Yield: 4 servings

Preheat the oven to 375°F (190°C, or gas mark 5). Line 2 baking sheets with parchment paper, lightly spritz with cooking spray, and set aside.

Set up a breading station: In one shallow dish, add the flour, ¼ teaspoon of salt, and pepper. Mix well. In another shallow dish, add the coconut milk. In a third shallow dish, add the panko bread crumbs, nutritional yeast, remaining ¼ teaspoon of salt, garlic powder, Italian seasoning, and oregano. Mix well.

Take a slice of the eggplant, dredge it in the flour and shake off any excess, and then dunk it in the coconut milk, letting any excess drip off. Then, place it in the bread crumbs, turning it over to ensure both sides are evenly covered, and place it on the prepared baking sheet. Repeat with the remaining slices of eggplant.

Bake for 15 minutes, gently flip each slice over, and then bake for another 10 minutes.

Meanwhile, cook the spaghetti noodles according to package directions. Make the Quick and Easy Marinara Sauce.

To serve: Plate the spaghetti noodles and Quick and Easy Marinara Sauce; you won't need all the sauce. Serve the eggplant on top. Top with additional Quick and Easy Marinara Sauce if desired.

SERVING SUGGESTION: Try it with zoodles (zucchini noodles) instead of traditional spaghetti!

Kids in the Kitchen
Have your kids get their hands messy and help with the breading!

Meaty Mushroom Stew
over Garlic Mashed Potatoes

This recipe reminds me a bit of pot roasts from my childhood. Of course, back then, it was beef, not mushrooms, but the flavor profiles are similar and both d ishes are warm comfort food that make me want to curl up on the couch with a big bowl.

FOR THE GARLIC MASHED POTATOES:

2 pounds (900 g) Yukon Gold potatoes, peeled and diced

½ teaspoon salt, or to taste

2 tablespoons (28 g) plant-based butter or (28 ml) extra-virgin olive oil

½ cup (120 ml) lite coconut milk, plus more as needed

½ teaspoon garlic powder, or to taste

FOR THE MEATY MUSHROOM STEW:

2 tablespoons (28 ml) olive oil

1 yellow onion, diced

2 cloves garlic, minced

2 carrots, peeled and diced

10 ounces (280 g) sliced cremini mushrooms

10 ounces (280 g) sliced shiitake mushrooms

1 tablespoon (16 g) tomato paste

2 tablespoons (28 ml) tamari, coconut aminos, or soy sauce (gluten-free, if desired)

2 teaspoons dried thyme

2 teaspoons dried sage

1½ teaspoons salt, or to taste

¼ teaspoon black pepper, or to taste

1½ cups (355 ml) low-sodium vegetable broth

1 cup (130 g) frozen green peas

Yield: 4 servings

For the Mashed Potatoes: Add the potatoes to a large pot on the stove. Cover the potatoes with water by 2 to 3 inches (5 to 7.5 cm). Add ½ teaspoon of salt. Turn the heat to high and bring to a boil and then reduce the heat to low. Simmer for 15 to 20 minutes until the potatoes are tender and easily pierced with a knife. Drain and add the potatoes back to the pot. Add the butter and coconut milk.

Using a potato masher, mash the potatoes until smooth. Add additional milk 1 tablespoon (15 ml) at a time if you like your mashed potatoes a thinner consistency. Add the garlic powder and additional salt to taste. Switch to a spatula or wooden spoon to stir and incorporate the seasonings well. Set aside.

For the Meaty Mushroom Stew: Meanwhile, heat the olive oil over medium heat in a large pan. Add the onion and sauté for 5 to 6 minutes until soft and translucent. Add the garlic and carrots and sauté for 2 to 3 minutes. Add the mushrooms and sauté for 8 to 10 minutes, stirring occasionally.

Add the tomato paste, tamari, thyme, sage, salt, pepper, and vegetable broth. Increase the heat to bring to a boil and then reduce the heat to low to simmer for 10 minutes. Add the green peas, stir to incorporate, and simmer for 1 to 2 minutes to heat through.

Serve the Meaty Mushroom Stew over the Garlic Mashed Potatoes.

Kids in the Kitchen
Kids love to mash potatoes!

Roasted Potato Wedges
with the World's Easiest Chili

This was another big winner among my recipe testers! Fat steak fries are roasted until crispy on the outside and tender on the inside and then topped with an incredibly quick black bean chili. It doesn't get much easier or more delicious. It's simplicity at its finest!

FOR THE ROASTED POTATO WEDGES:

4 large Yukon Gold potatoes, cut into wedges (peeled, if desired)

1 tablespoon (15 ml) olive oil

1 teaspoon dried oregano

½ teaspoon garlic powder

½ teaspoon paprika

¼ teaspoon salt, or to taste

⅛ teaspoon black pepper, or to taste

FOR THE WORLD'S EASIEST CHILI:

2 cans (15 ounces or 425 g each) black beans, drained and rinsed (or 3 cups [516 g] cooked beans)

1 jar (12 ounces, or 340 g) tomato-based salsa

1 tablespoon (8 g) chili powder

1 teaspoon cumin

½ cup (120 ml) low-sodium vegetable broth

FOR SERVING:

BEST Guacamole (page 162)

Yield: 4 servings

Preheat the oven to 400°F (200°C, or gas mark 6). Line a rimmed baking sheet with parchment paper and set aside.

For the Roasted Potato Wedges: Toss the potato wedges with the olive oil and spices. Spread out in one even layer on the prepared baking sheet. Roast for 20 minutes, flip over, and roast for another 10 to 15 minutes until golden brown and tender.

For the World's Easiest Chili: Meanwhile, add all the chili ingredients to a pot over medium-high heat. Bring to a boil and then reduce the heat to medium-low. Simmer for 10 to 15 minutes until thick and bubbly. With a potato masher, mash half of the black beans, if desired, to create a thicker sauce.

Serve the World's Easiest Chili over the Roasted Potato Wedges and top with a dollop of BEST Guacamole.

Kids in the Kitchen
Have the kids toss the potatoes wedges in the olive oil and spices and then make the chili.

Butternut Squash–Quinoa Patties
with Lemon Cashew Aioli and the BEST Roasted Broccoli

These patties are firm and crispy on the outside, but tender and creamy on the inside. A bit of butternut squash—quinoa patty, a bit of broccoli, and a drizzle of aioli all in one bite—it's heaven!

FOR THE PATTIES:

2 cups (280 g) peeled and diced butternut squash

1 red onion, halved and sliced

1 tablespoon (15 ml) olive oil

¼ teaspoon salt, or to taste

⅛ teaspoon black pepper, or to taste

¾ cup (175 ml) water

½ cup (87 g) dry quinoa, rinsed well

2 tablespoons (32 g) tomato paste

2 teaspoons Dijon mustard

Juice of ½ lemon

1 teaspoon dried thyme

½ teaspoon ground sage

¼ cup (13 g) panko bread crumbs

Cooking spray

FOR THE BROCCOLI:

2 heads broccoli, chopped into florets

1 tablespoon (15 ml) olive oil

¼ teaspoon salt, or to taste

⅛ teaspoon black pepper, or to taste

FOR THE LEMON CASHEW AIOLI (MAKES ABOUT ¾ CUP [175 G]):

½ cup (70 g) raw cashews

½ cup (120 ml) water

1 tablespoon (15 ml) fresh lemon juice

1 clove garlic

1 teaspoon dried thyme

1 teaspoon ground sage

½ teaspoon onion powder

½ teaspoon salt, or to taste

Yield: 4 servings

Preheat the oven to 400°F (200°C, or gas mark 6). Line a rimmed baking sheet with parchment paper and set aside.

For the Patties: Toss the butternut squash, onion, olive oil, salt, and pepper in a large bowl. Mix well. Spread onto the prepared baking sheet in one even layer. Roast for 15 minutes, stir, and roast for another 15 minutes until the squash is tender.

Meanwhile, bring the water to a boil in a small pot on the stove. Add the quinoa and stir. Reduce heat to a simmer and cover. Cook for 12 to 15 minutes until the water is absorbed and the quinoa is tender.

Add the roasted squash and onions and the quinoa to a food processor with the tomato paste, Dijon mustard, lemon juice, thyme, sage, and panko bread crumbs. Pulse several times to combine, scraping down the sides as necessary. Do not overprocess into a purée. You should still be able to see some chunks of squash and red onion. Turn out into a bowl and make sure the bread crumbs are distributed evenly. Divide the mixture into 4 equal sections and shape them into patties.

Heat a large nonstick skillet over medium heat and spray gently with cooking spray. Add the patties, leaving space between each one. Cook for 15 minutes or so on the first side. A thin spatula should slide easily underneath when the patties are ready to be turned. If it doesn't, let them cook a minute or two longer. Flip and cook for another 10 to 15 minutes on the second side. You may need to respray your pan with cooking spray when you flip them. You may also need to adjust the heat if your patties are browning too quickly or don't seem to be browning enough.

For the Broccoli: Toss the broccoli with olive oil, salt, and pepper. Remove the sheet of parchment you used to roast the squash and onions and add a new sheet. Spread the broccoli out in one even layer. Roast for 15 minutes, stir, and roast for 10 to 15 minutes more until the tops of the broccoli are starting to brown.

For the Lemon Cashew Aioli: Add all the ingredients to a high-speed blender. Purée until smooth.

To serve, plate one Butternut Squash–Quinoa Patty, a spoonful of The BEST Roasted Broccoli, and drizzle a few tablespoons (40 g) of Lemon Cashew Aioli over everything.

Cheesy Broccoli Stuffed Baked Potatoes

I've used broccoli in this recipe, but you can use whatever vegetables you prefer. Cauliflower would be delicious, as would sweet green peas, asparagus, or Brussels sprouts. Drenched in the creamy Butternut Mac Cheese Sauce, the kids won't care which veggies are under there. The whole thing is topped off with addictively crunchy roasted chickpeas—and they are a great snack on their own, by the way!

4 large russet potatoes, scrubbed well and dried

1 can (15 ounces, or 425 g) chickpeas, drained and rinsed (or 1½ cups [246 g] cooked chickpeas)

1 head broccoli, cut into florets

2 tablespoons (28 ml) olive oil, divided

1 teaspoon Italian seasoning

¼ teaspoon garlic powder

¼ teaspoon paprika

¾ teaspoon salt, divided, or to taste

⅛ teaspoon black pepper

1 recipe Butternut Mac Cheese Sauce (page 167)

Yield: 4 servings

Preheat the oven to 425°F (220°C, or gas mark 7). Line a rimmed baking sheet with parchment paper and set aside.

Pierce the potatoes several times using a fork. Wrap the potatoes in aluminum foil and place directly on the oven racks. Bake for 50 to 60 minutes until soft.

In a medium-size mixing bowl, toss the chickpeas with 1 tablespoon (15 ml) of olive oil, Italian seasoning, garlic powder, paprika, and ½ teaspoon of salt. Mix well. Transfer to one half of the baking sheet in an even layer.

Using the same mixing bowl, toss the broccoli florets with 1 tablespoon (15 ml) of olive oil, ¼ teaspoon of salt, and pepper. Mix well. Transfer to the other half of the baking sheet in an even layer.

When there is 20 minutes left of baking time for the potatoes, put the chickpeas and broccoli into the oven. Bake for 15 minutes, shake the pans, and bake for 5 to 10 minutes more until the chickpeas are crunchy and the broccoli tips are browned.

To serve, make a slit in the tops of the potatoes lengthwise and gently press the two ends toward each other to open the potatoes. Place a scoop of broccoli and a spoonful or two of chickpeas on each potato. Drizzle with a generous amount of Butternut Mac Cheese Sauce.

Roasted Cauliflower Tacos
with Pineapple Salsa and Chipotle Cream

If you're looking for a taco that's HUGE on flavor and texture, this is it! The pineapple salsa is a kid favorite in our house. Sometimes, we add diced avocado to the salsa as well at their request.

FOR THE ROASTED CAULIFLOWER:

1 head cauliflower, chopped into bite-size florets (about 4 cups [500 g])

1 tablespoon (15 ml) olive oil

1 tablespoon (15 ml) fresh lime juice

1 teaspoon chili powder

1 teaspoon cumin

½ teaspoon smoked paprika

¾ teaspoon salt, or to taste

¼ teaspoon garlic powder

⅛ teaspoon black pepper

FOR THE PINEAPPLE SALSA:

1 can (20 ounces, or 560 g) pineapple tidbits (If you can only find pineapple chunks, cut them into quarters.)

1 jalapeño, ribs and seeds removed, diced

2 tablespoons (20 g) diced red onion

Juice of 1 lime

⅛ teaspoon salt, or to taste

FOR THE CHIPOTLE CREAM:

½ cup (70 g) raw cashews

1–2 chipotle peppers in adobo (Start with 1; add another if you like it spicier.)

1 tablespoon (15 ml) apple cider vinegar

⅔ cup (175 ml) pineapple juice from the can of pineapple tidbits used above (plus more to thin)

¼ teaspoon salt, or to taste

Preheat the oven to 400°F (200°C, or gas mark 6). Line a rimmed baking sheet with parchment paper and set aside.

Place the cashews for the Chipotle Cream in a bowl. Cover with hot water. Set aside to soak.

In a mixing bowl, toss the cauliflower florets with the olive oil, lime juice, chili powder, cumin, smoked paprika, salt, garlic powder, and pepper. Spread out in one even layer on the prepared baking sheet. Bake for 20 minutes, stir, and bake for another 10 to 15 minutes until the cauliflower is tender and the edges are crispy.

For the Pineapple Salsa: Meanwhile, drain the can of pineapple over a bowl to reserve the juice. Set the pineapple juice aside. Add the pineapple tidbits to a bowl and add the remaining salsa ingredients. Toss to combine.

To make the Chipotle Cream, drain and rinse the soaked cashews. Add them to a blender along with the reserved pineapple juice, 1 chipotle in adobo sauce, apple cider vinegar, and salt. Blend until smooth. Taste and add another chipotle in adobo sauce if you want it spicier and blend again.

Kids in the Kitchen
Have the kids break the cauliflower into florets and toss them with the spices. They can help assemble the tacos as well.

FOR THE TACOS:

Shredded cabbage or coleslaw mix

Chopped cilantro (optional)

8 taco-size tortillas (gluten-free, if desired)

Yield: 4 servings

For the Tacos: Place some shredded cabbage and cilantro, if using, on a tortilla. Add several pieces of Roasted Cauliflower, ¼ cup (about 65 g) of Pineapple Salsa, and a drizzle of Chipotle Cream. Repeat with the remaining ingredients.

NOTE: Chipotles in adobo can be quite spicy. The cashews and pineapple juice help to tame the heat in the sauce, but if you're serving small children, be sure to start with just one and only add more after tasting for heat level.

Thai Sweet Potato Curry

I love anything with sweet potatoes and my kids love anything with peanut butter, so this dish is what we call a win-win. Their bowls are definitely more rice-heavy than mine, but I'm okay with that. It's all about balance.

1½ tablespoons (23 g) coconut oil

1 yellow onion, diced

2 cloves garlic, minced

3-4 tablespoons (45-60 g) Thai red curry paste

2 sweet potatoes, peeled and diced (about 3 cups or 400 g)

1 can (15 ounces, or 425 g) diced tomatoes

1 cup (235 ml) low-sodium vegetable broth

2 teaspoon salt, divided

¼ teaspoon black pepper

¼ cup (65 g) smooth natural peanut butter

½ cup (120 ml) lite coconut milk

2 tablespoons (2 g) chopped cilantro

Juice of 1 lime

3 cups (474 g) cooked jasmine rice or rice of your choice

¼ cup (36 g) chopped peanuts, for garnish

Yield: 4 servings

Heat the coconut oil in pot or large skillet over medium heat. Add the onion and sauté for 5 to 6 minutes until soft and translucent. Add the garlic and red curry paste and stir until fully incorporated with the onions. Add the sweet potatoes, tomatoes, vegetable broth, 1 teaspoon of salt, and pepper. Increase the heat to high and bring to a boil and then reduce the heat to medium-low. Simmer for 30 to 35 minutes until the sweet potatoes are fork tender.

In a small cup or bowl, whisk together the peanut butter, coconut milk, and remaining 1 of teaspoon of salt. Pour into the skillet with the sweet potatoes and stir to combine.

Remove from the heat. Add the cilantro and lime juice. Serve with the cooked rice and garnish with the chopped peanuts.

Tex-Mex Stuffed Peppers

Bell peppers are one of the most popular vegetables in our house. The kids happily take sliced bell peppers in their lunch boxes several times a week, and I cook with them often. We make a lot of stuffed peppers in the summer when our garden plants are flourishing. I have a Mediterranean version with a dreamy red pepper sauce on the blog if you want more stuffed pepper goodness.

1 tablespoon (15 ml) olive oil

½ yellow onion, diced

1½ teaspoons smoked paprika

1½ teaspoons cumin

¼ teaspoon salt

1 cup (155 g) dry instant brown rice (see note)

¼ cup (60 ml) water, plus enough to cook the rice, divided

1 can (15 ounces, or 425 g) pinto beans or black beans, rinsed and drained (or 1½ cups [258 g] cooked beans)

1 cup (164 g) fresh or frozen corn kernels

1 can (15 ounces, or 425 g) diced tomatoes, drained

¼ cup (4 g) cilantro, chopped

Juice of 1 lime

4 bell peppers, halved, seeds and ribs removed (red, orange, or yellow)

½ cup (125 g) Sharp Salsa Queso Dip (page 167)

Creamy Cumin Ranch Dressing (page 162; optional)

Yield: 4 to 6 servings

Preheat the oven to 400°F (200°C, or gas mark 6).

Heat the olive oil over medium heat in a pot on the stove. Add the onion and sauté for 5 to 6 minutes until soft and translucent. Add the smoked paprika, cumin, and salt and sauté for 1 minute until fragrant.

Add the rice and amount of water indicated for 1 cup (155 g) of rice on the package directions; stir. Bring to a boil, cover, reduce the heat to low, and simmer for 5 to 10 minutes (or the length of time indicated on rice package directions) until tender. Add the beans, corn, drained tomatoes, cilantro, and lime juice. Stir well. Remove from the heat.

Pour the remaining ¼ cup (60 ml) of water into the bottom of a 9- × 13-inch (23 × 33 cm) baking dish. Place the bell peppers cut-side up in the dish. Spread 1 tablespoon of Sharp Salsa Queso Dip in each pepper. Fill each pepper with about ½ cup (268 g) of the rice-bean mixture. If you have any leftover filing, just sprinkle it over the top.

Bake for 20 minutes until the peppers are tender. Drizzle with the Creamy Cumin Ranch Dressing, if desired.

Kids in the Kitchen

The kids can drain and rinse the beans, and they can fill the peppers.

CHAPTER 10

Breakfast for Dinner

Just as we sometimes eat dinner leftovers for breakfast, we occasionally bring out the breakfast vibes for dinner. There is certainly no law that says you have to eat breakfast-type foods before noon. I often add pancakes to my kids' lunch boxes and oatmeal to their thermoses, too. And who doesn't love a good PB&J for dinner from time to time? This busy mom sure does!

The Best Oatmeal Bowl

This recipe is really more about the method and a few basic ingredients. The toppings are what's going to make it your own. And you can switch up your toppings to make a different version every time, so you never get bored. But stick with this basic method and, trust me, you will fall in love with oatmeal!

FOR THE OATMEAL:

3¼ cups (760 g) cold water

2 ripe bananas, smashed well (Use just one if you are not a banana lover.)

2 cups (160 g) old-fashioned rolled oats

2 heaping tablespoons (about 40 g) peanut butter or almond butter

½ teaspoon ground cinnamon (optional)

TOPPINGS:

Extra dollop of nut butter

Sprinkle of chopped nuts or seeds (We like hemp seeds.)

Fresh fruit

Dried fruit

Spices such as cinnamon, nutmeg, or ginger

Dairy-free chocolate chips

Granola

Pure maple syrup

Yield: 4 servings

Mash the bananas with a fork until they resemble a purée.

Add the water to a pot on the stove. Whisk in the banana until well incorporated.

Add the oats to the cold water and then turn on the stove to medium-high. As soon as the oatmeal comes to a simmer, add the peanut butter and cinnamon, if using, turn down the heat to low, and cook until the desired consistency, stirring occasionally. This generally takes less than 10 minutes.

Spoon into individual bowls. Top with (or stir in) your ingredients of choice.

SERVING SUGGESTIONS: Some of our favorite combos are: peanut butter, diced apple, cinnamon, and hemp seeds; almond butter, frozen blueberries, a dash of powdered ginger, and a drizzle of pure maple syrup; and peanut butter, fresh sliced banana, dairy-free chocolate chips, and shredded coconut.

Swap It!

For a gluten-free version, make sure to choose certified gluten-free oats.

For a nut-free version, use sunflower seed butter instead of nut butter.

Garlicky White Bean Avocado Toast
with BBQ Drizzle

If you didn't think avocado toast could get any better, it just did! I eat this for lunch often as it's easy to scale down (or up!). With such a short ingredient list, you'll be amazed at how delicious this is!

1 tablespoon (15 ml) olive oil

3 cloves garlic, minced

1 can (15 ounces, or 425 g) cannellini beans (white kidney beans), drained and rinsed (or 1½ cups [269 g] cooked beans)

½ teaspoon dried oregano

½ teaspoon salt, or to taste

Pinch of black pepper, or to taste

2 avocados, peeled and pits removed

4 slices hearty whole-grain bread, toasted (gluten-free, if desired)

Sweet-and-Spicy BBQ Sauce (page 165) or store-bought BBQ sauce

Hemp seeds, for garnish

Yield: 4 servings

Heat the olive oil over medium heat in a small skillet. Add the garlic. Sauté for 1 to 2 minutes; watch it carefully so it doesn't burn and turn down the heat a bit if necessary. Add the cannellini beans, oregano, salt, and pepper and sauté for 4 to 5 minutes until hot.

To serve: Mash ½ of an avocado on each slice of toast. Spoon one-quarter of the bean mixture over the mashed avocado on each slice. Drizzle with BBQ sauce and sprinkle with hemp seeds.

SERVING SUGGESTION: We like this with a side of fresh fruit to offset the richness of the avocado and beans.

Kids in the Kitchen

Have the kids drain and rinse the beans, mash the avocado, and toast the bread.

Oatmeal Cookie Granola Parfait

Here's a breakfast that tastes like dessert! We are a little obsessed with granola in our house. We eat it for breakfast, snacks, and dessert. Throw it in a container and take it on-the-go. Pack it in a lunch box. Or layer it up with yogurt and fruit and make a pretty parfait!

FOR THE OATMEAL COOKIE GRANOLA (MAKES ABOUT 2 CUPS [220 G]):

1½ cups (120 g) old-fashioned rolled oats

1 cup (30 g) crisp brown rice cereal

½ cup (160 g) pure maple syrup

1 teaspoon pure vanilla extract

1½ teaspoons ground cinnamon

¼ teaspoon salt

¼ cup (35 g) raisins, (60 g) dairy-free chocolate chips, or both (optional)

FOR THE PARFAIT:

2 cups (460 g) plain or flavored plant-based yogurt

2 cups (weight will vary) fruit (blueberries, sliced strawberries, diced apple, etc.)

Yield: 4 servings

For the Oatmeal Cookie Granola: Preheat the oven to 300°F (150°C, or gas mark 2). Line a rimmed baking sheet with parchment paper and set aside.

Combine the oats and crisp brown rice cereal in a mixing bowl.

In a small bowl or cup, whisk together the maple syrup, vanilla, cinnamon, and salt.

Pour the wet ingredients over the dry ingredients while stirring to incorporate. Mix well to ensure all the dry ingredients are coated.

Spread out onto the prepared baking sheet into one compact even layer. Pat it down, but don't spread it out too much, you don't want gaps in between.

Bake for 30 minutes. I like to turn my pan around in the oven at the 20-minute mark to ensure even cooking because our oven does have some hot spots. DO NOT STIR during the cooking time. Let it cool on the pan for about 10 minutes and then break into clumps. Let the granola continue to cool completely.

Stir in the raisins or chocolate chips, or both, if using.

To assemble the parfaits: Dollop some yogurt in the bottom of a glass or small bowl. Top with a sprinkle of granola and some fruit. Repeat 2 or 3 times for each parfait. If preparing in advance, put all the granola on top or in a separate container and mix when ready to serve.

Kids in the Kitchen

The kids can mix up the granola and assemble the parfaits.

Banana Walnut Baked Oatmeal

You should make this baked oatmeal just for the kitchen smells alone—rich bananas, sweet cinnamon and maple syrup, and nutty oats and walnuts. It's best served warm with fresh sliced bananas and an extra drizzle of syrup.

3 cups (240 g) old-fashioned rolled oats (gluten-free, if desired)

2 tablespoons (14 g) flaxseed meal (ground flaxseeds)

1½ teaspoons baking powder

1 teaspoon ground cinnamon

½ teaspoon salt

½ cup (50 g) raw walnuts, chopped

1 ripe banana, mashed

½ cup (160 g) pure maple syrup, plus more for serving

1 cup (235 ml) unsweetened plain almond milk or milk of choice

½ teaspoon pure vanilla extract

Fresh banana slices, for topping

Hemp seeds, for topping

Yield: 6 servings

Preheat the oven to 350°F (180°C, or gas mark 4). Line an 8- × 8- (20 × 20 cm) baking dish with parchment paper or spray it lightly with cooking spray. Set aside.

In a large mixing bowl, stir together the oats, flaxseed meal, baking powder, cinnamon, salt, and walnuts.

In a small mixing bowl, whisk together the banana, maple syrup, almond milk, and vanilla.

Pour the wet ingredients into the dry ingredients. Stir well to combine, scraping down the sides of the bowl as necessary to ensure everything is coated.

Pour the mixture in the prepared baking dish. Bake for 25 to 30 minutes until set.

Let cool for 10 minutes before cutting and serving.

Top with fresh sliced banana, a sprinkle of hemp seeds, and an extra drizzle of pure maple syrup, if desired.

NOTE: For a nut-free version, leave out the walnuts.

Add It!
For extra indulgence, add ½ cup (87 g) of dairy-free chocolate chips.

Kids in the Kitchen
Kids can make most of this recipe themselves, from measuring the ingredients, mashing the banana, and mixing it all together.

Peanut Butter Pancakes
with Maple–Peanut Butter Syrup

If you love peanut butter, this recipe is for you! There's peanut butter in the pancakes and peanut butter in the syrup. It's sweet and indulgent and oh-so-good!

FOR THE PEANUT BUTTER PANCAKES:

1½ cups (180 g) spelt flour or (188 g) all-purpose flour

2 teaspoons baking powder

½ teaspoon salt

¼ teaspoon ground cinnamon (optional)

½ cup (130 g) organic natural peanut butter

1¾ cup (410 ml) unsweetened plain almond milk or milk of choice

3 tablespoons (60 g) pure maple syrup

1 teaspoon pure vanilla extract

Cooking spray

FOR THE MAPLE–PEANUT BUTTER SYRUP:

¼ cup (65 g) organic natural peanut butter

2 tablespoons (40 g) pure maple syrup

4–6 tablespoons (60–90 ml) unsweetened plain almond milk or milk of choice

¼ teaspoon pure vanilla extract (optional)

Dash of cinnamon (optional)

TOPPINGS (OPTIONAL):

Banana slices

Dairy-Free chocolate chips

Chopped raw peanuts

4 to 6 servings

For the Peanut Butter Pancakes: In a large mixing bowl, whisk together the flour, baking powder, salt, and cinnamon, if using.

In a large measuring cup, whisk together the peanut butter, almond milk, maple syrup, and vanilla.

Pour the wet ingredients into the dry ingredients and stir until just combined. Set aside for about 10 minutes to let the batter thicken up.

Lightly spray a nonstick skillet with cooking spray and heat over medium heat. Once hot, pour ¼ cup (60 ml) of batter for each pancake. Do not crowd the pan; I do two at a time. You might be able to fit three if you have a large pan.

Cook each pancake for about 3 to 5 minutes. It's ready to flip when the edges start turning lightly brown and bubbles begin to pop on top of the pancake. Gently flip and cook for another 3 to 5 minutes. Transfer to a plate and continue until all the batter has been used. You might need to add additional cooking spray before adding each new batch to the pan. You also may need to adjust the heat as you go. The pan will get hotter the longer you use it, so just watch your pancakes and turn down the heat a bit if necessary.

For the Maple–Peanut Butter Syrup: Whisk together all the ingredients listed. Try not to drink it before your pancakes are ready—it's so darn good!

Serve the Peanut Butter Pancakes with any of the optional toppings, if desired, and a good drizzle of the Maple Peanut-Butter Syrup.

Kids in the Kitchen

Kids can mix the batter and whisk the syrup. They can even flip the pancakes (younger kids may need help).

Tofu Scramble
with Avocado Salsa and Toast

Soft tofu scrambles up with a look and texture that is shockingly similar to scrambled eggs. I add a bit of turmeric to enhance the yellow color and just enough spices and veggies to season it up, but the tofu is the star here. Served with the Avocado Salsa, you've got a winner of a dish for any time of day!

FOR THE TOFU SCRAMBLE:

1 package (14 ounces, or 390 g) soft tofu (NOT silken)

2 tablespoons (28 ml) olive oil

¼ cup (40 g) diced red onion

½ green bell pepper, seeded and diced

1 clove garlic, minced

½ teaspoon cumin

½ teaspoon salt, or to taste

¼ teaspoon black pepper, or to taste

¼ teaspoon ground turmeric, plus more for a deeper color if desired

FOR THE AVOCADO SALSA:

1 avocado, peel and pit removed, diced

1 pint (275 g) grape tomatoes, halved or quartered

¼ cup (40 g) diced red onion

Juice of 1 lime

¼ teaspoon salt, or to taste

1 tablespoon (1 g) chopped fresh cilantro

Yield: 4 servings

For the Tofu Scramble: Wrap the block of tofu in several paper towels or a clean kitchen towel and place on a plate. Place another plate on top of the tofu and weigh down the top plate. Cans or bags of beans or rice work well for this or a heavy skillet. This tower may start to topple as the tofu loses liquid, so don't use anything breakable, like glass jars, as a weight. Press for at least 20 minutes.

Heat the olive oil in a skillet over medium heat. Add the onion and bell pepper. Sauté for 5 to 6 minutes until the onion is soft and translucent. Add the garlic and spices and stir well to combine.

Using your clean hands, crumble the tofu into the pan. Vary the size of the pieces you break off so that they resemble the texture of scrambled eggs. Stir to mix well. The tofu should take on a yellow color from the turmeric. Add a pinch more of turmeric if you want a deeper color. Cook for 4 to 5 minutes until the tofu is heated through.

For the Avocado Salsa: Combine all the ingredients in a small bowl. Mix well to combine.

Serve the Tofu Scramble with a scoop of Avocado Salsa on the side.

SERVING SUGGESTION: Serve with whole-grain toast.

Chickpea Scramble Breakfast Burrito

Protein-packed chickpeas mingle with Tex-Mex spices and superfood spinach all cozy-like in a big ol' burrito. This chickpea scramble is just as good on its own as it is stuffed into a tortilla. Try it both ways!

1 tablespoon (15 ml) olive oil

½ yellow onion, diced

½ red bell pepper, seeded and diced

2 cloves garlic, minced

1 teaspoon chili powder, or more to taste

½ teaspoon cumin

½ teaspoon ground turmeric

½ teaspoon salt, or to taste

¼ teaspoon black pepper, or to taste

1 can (15 ounces, or 425 g) chickpeas, drained and rinsed (or 1½ cups [246 g] cooked chickpeas)

Juice of ½ lemon

2 tablespoons (8 g) nutritional yeast (optional)

2 cups (60 g) fresh spinach, well chopped

4 large burrito-size tortillas (gluten-free, if desired)

½ cup (130 g) salsa

1 avocado, peel and pit removed, sliced

Yield: 4 servings

Heat the olive oil over medium heat in a large skillet. Add the onion and sauté for 5 to 6 minutes until soft and translucent. Add the bell pepper and garlic and sauté for 3 to 4 minutes until starting to soften.

Add the chili powder, cumin, turmeric, salt, and pepper. Sauté for 1 to 2 minutes until fragrant.

Add the chickpeas. Using a potato masher or a fork, mash about half of the chickpeas. Add the lemon juice and nutritional yeast, if using. Simmer for 5 to 10 minutes until some of the liquid has absorbed and the mixture is thick. Add the spinach and stir to combine. Sauté for 1 to 2 minutes to slightly wilt the spinach.

Wrap the tortillas in a just-damp paper towel and heat in the microwave for 20 to 30 seconds at a time until warm. Lay one tortilla flat and add one-quarter of the chickpea scramble on one end. On top of the scramble, add 2 tablespoons (33 g) of salsa and a few slices of avocado. Fold up the bottom half of the tortilla over the filling, then fold in both sides, and then starting from the bottom, tightly roll up the tortilla to form the burrito. Repeat with the remaining ingredients.

Swap It!
You may use gluten-free tortillas if desired but note that corn tortillas don't bend well and may break.

Oven-Baked Potato Hash

A pan full of roasted potatoes? Yes, please! This dish is so deliciously addictive that my kids stand around the hot pan on the stove picking off pieces before I even fill their plates.

3–5 russet potatoes, scrubbed well and diced into bite-size pieces (about 5 cups [550 g])

4 tablespoons (60 ml) olive oil, divided

2 teaspoons dried oregano

1 teaspoon paprika

1¼ teaspoon salt, or to taste, divided

½ teaspoon black pepper, or to taste, divided

1 yellow onion, diced

1 green bell pepper, seeded and diced

1 zucchini, chopped

Diced avocado, for serving (optional)

Salsa, for serving (optional)

Creamy Cumin Ranch Dressing (page 162; optional)

Yield: 4 servings

Preheat the oven to 425°F (220°C, or gas mark 7). Line a rimmed baking sheet with parchment paper and set aside.

In a large mixing bowl, toss the potatoes with 3 tablespoons (45 ml) of olive oil, oregano, paprika, 1 teaspoon of salt, and ¼ teaspoon of pepper. Spread out in one even layer on the prepared baking sheet. Bake for 20 minutes.

Meanwhile, toss the onion, bell pepper, and zucchini with remaining 1 tablespoon (15 ml) of olive oil, ¼ teaspoon of salt, and ¼ teaspoon of pepper.

After the potatoes bake for 20 minutes, add the veggies to the potatoes on the baking sheet and stir well. Bake for another 15 to 20 minutes until the potatoes are crispy on the outsides and tender on the insides.

Serve with diced avocado, a dollop of salsa, and a drizzle of Creamy Cumin Ranch Dressing, if desired.

Add It!

We love this as is with no added protein . . . it's a carb-lover's dream. Feel free to add a can of drained and rinsed black beans to the mix when you add the peppers and zucchini. Or, serve it up next to some Addictive Chewy Baked Tofu (page 168).

CHAPTER 11

Sauces and Staples

You know what they say: The sauce makes the meal! I wholeheartedly believe this. A good sauce can bring individual components of a dish into a composed meal. It's the tie that binds it all together. In addition to sauces and dressings, you'll find a few key recipes here that are used throughout this book many times.

Creamy Cumin Ranch Dressing

Here's a creamy, tangy, herby, dairy-free ranch dressing with a hint of southwest flavors. This dressing is super versatile! Try it on salads, burgers, baked potatoes, stirred into soup, as a dip for raw veggies or French fries . . . the possibilities are endless! It's one of the most popular recipes on my blog.

¾ cup (105 g) raw cashews (soaked for 1–2 hours if you don't have a high-speed blender, then drained)

½ cup (120 ml) water, plus more to thin if needed

Juice of 1 lemon

1 tablespoon (15 ml) apple cider vinegar

1 clove garlic

1 teaspoon cumin

1 teaspoon dried dill

1 teaspoon snipped chives

½ teaspoon smoked paprika

½ teaspoon onion powder

½ teaspoon dried oregano

½ teaspoon salt, or to taste

Yield: about 1¼ cups (295 ml)

Blend all the ingredients in a high-speed blender until smooth. Add additional water 1 tablespoon (15 ml) at a time, if necessary, to thin.

BEST Guacamole

Guacamole is life. Just a few simple ingredients bring so much flavor and texture. It's creamy, yet chunky, tangy, and spicy. My friend's husband, a chef at a downtown Chicago hot spot, proclaimed this guacamole recipe as the best, and who am I to disagree with an actual chef?! Make it and put it on everything!

4 avocados, pits and peels removed

1 Roma tomato, diced

2–3 tablespoons (20–30 g) diced red onion

¼ cup (4 g) cilantro, chopped

Juice of 1 lime

Salt

1–2 jalapeños, ribs and seeds removed, diced

Yield: about 3 cups (675 g)

In a medium bowl, mash the avocado with a fork or potato masher until smooth.

Add all the other ingredients and use 2 jalapeños if you like spicy! Stir to combine. Taste and adjust the seasoning, if necessary.

Serve immediately.

Kids in the Kitchen

Hand your kids the potato masher and have them get to work mashing the avocado while you chop the rest of the ingredients.

Citrus Tahini Dressing

This creamy salad dressing celebrates tahini in all its glory. It has a slight bitterness, but the citrus juice balances it out nicely. If you prefer a sweeter dressing, you can add a tablespoon (20 g) of pure maple syrup, but we love it just the way it is. It's the perfect drizzle for all your leafy greens . . . and so much more! Try it on roasted vegetables, falafel, tacos, lentils and rice, anything! Bonus: It's oil-free!

⅓ cup (80 g) tahini

¼ cup (60 ml) fresh squeezed orange juice

2 tablespoons (28 ml) apple cider vinegar

¼ teaspoon salt, or to taste

1–2 tablespoons (15–28 ml) water to thin, if needed

Whisk all the ingredients in a jar or bowl until smooth.

Yield: about ¾ to 1 cup (175 to 235 ml)

Maple Dijon Vinaigrette

Don't buy pricey store-bought vinaigrettes with questionable ingredients. This sweet and tangy dressing is incredibly easy to make, and it is made from pantry staples. It will become a staple in your fridge, too.

3 tablespoons (45 g) Dijon mustard

2 tablespoons (40 g) pure maple syrup, or to taste

2 tablespoons (28 ml) apple cider vinegar

½ teaspoon salt, or to taste

½ cup (120 ml) extra-virgin olive oil

In a small bowl, whisk together all the ingredients until smooth.

Yield: about 1 cup (235 ml)

Mixed Greens Pepita Pesto

This pesto has so much flavor! It's bright and vibrant. The pumpkin seeds (pepitas) have a "cheesy" flavor that replaces Parmesan cheese perfectly. Because pine nuts and I do not get along, I always use almonds. Whenever I take this pesto to parties as a dip, it's gone in minutes. Everyone loves it!

1 cup (about 24 g) packed fresh basil leaves

1 cup (about 20 g) packed arugula

2 cloves garlic, peeled

½ cup (70 g) raw shelled pumpkin seeds (pepitas)

¼ cup (36 g) raw almonds

¼ cup (60 ml) fresh lemon juice

½ teaspoon salt, or to taste

⅛ teaspoon black pepper, or to taste

2 tablespoons (28 ml) extra-virgin olive oil

2–3 tablespoons (28–45 ml) water, to thin

Yield: 1½ cups (390 g)

In a food processor, place the basil, arugula, garlic, pumpkin seeds, almonds, lemon juice, salt, and pepper. With the food processor running, drizzle in the extra-virgin olive oil through the top. Stop and scrape down the sides and process again to incorporate. Through the top with the food processor running, add the water 1 tablespoon (15 ml) at a time until the desired consistency is reached.

Kids in the Kitchen

Your kids can probably make this recipe on their own. Watch them carefully as they scrape down the sides of the food processor as the blades inside are very sharp!

Quick and Easy Marinara Sauce

This marinara recipe tastes like a sauce you'd get in a restaurant, yet it's so easy to make and is ready in just twenty minutes! My kids will practically eat this sauce with a spoon. This recipe makes a lot because it goes well with so many different dishes. Cook once, eat twice (or more)! Use it on pasta and pizza or as a dip for quesadillas or garlic bread. Add it to soup, rice, or stuffed peppers. Leftovers will keep in the fridge for several days and in the freezer for up to 6 months, but feel free to halve the recipe if you wish.

1 can (28 ounces, or 785 g) crushed tomatoes

1 can (15 ounces, or 425 g) tomato sauce

¼ cup (64 g) tomato paste

1 teaspoon salt, or to taste

1 teaspoon dried basil

1 teaspoon dried oregano

½ teaspoon garlic powder

½ teaspoon onion powder

1 teaspoon granulated organic white sugar

Yield: 5 cups (1.2 L)

Add all the ingredients to a pot over medium heat on the stove. When it begins to bubble, turn the heat down to low and simmer for 15 to 20 minutes. Add additional salt or seasonings to taste, if necessary.

Sweet-and-Spicy BBQ Sauce

A little sweet and a little heat balance perfectly in this easy blender sauce. It will make you want to slather everything in BBQ sauce!

6 ounces (170 g) tomato paste

¼ cup (60 ml) apple cider vinegar

¼ cup (60 ml) balsamic vinegar

3 tablespoons (60 g) pure maple syrup

1–2 chipotle peppers in adobo

1 teaspoon smoked paprika

1 teaspoon ground mustard

½ teaspoon onion powder

¼ teaspoon garlic powder

½ teaspoon salt, or to taste

½ cup (120 ml) water, to thin, or more as needed

Yield: 1½ cups (355 ml)

Place all the ingredients into a blender; use 2 chipotle peppers if you like it spicier. Purée until smooth.

Transfer sauce to a pot over medium-high heat and bring to a boil and then reduce the heat to low. Simmer for 15 to 20 minutes until thick, or until the desired consistency is reached.

Romesco Sauce

This sauce is like a pesto in texture but made with peppers. Many versions are thickened with leftover bread, but here I'm using panko bread crumbs because they're a pantry staple and they help create that wonderful pesto-like texture. My version is smoky and a little sweet, and it pairs well with a variety of dishes. Try it on pasta or rice. Use it as a dip for garlic bread or quesadillas or simply drizzle it over roasted vegetables.

1 jar (12 ounces, or 340 g) roasted red peppers, drained

1 can (15 ounces, or 425 g) fired roasted diced tomatoes, drained

½ cup (73 g) raw almonds

¼ cup (13 g) panko bread crumbs or regular bread crumbs

2 cloves garlic

1 tablespoon (7 g) smoked paprika

½ teaspoon salt, or to taste

1 tablespoon (15 ml) balsamic vinegar

Yield: about 3 cups (700 ml)

Place all the ingredients in a food processor. Process until mostly smooth. It should resemble a pesto in texture, so it won't be totally smooth.

Sharp Salsa Queso Dip

This may seem like an odd mix of ingredients, but trust me, you are going to LOVE this dip! It tastes like sharp pub cheese, but with a salsa twist. All my testers loved it, and the kids couldn't believe it didn't contain cheese.

1 cup (140 g) raw cashews

¼ cup (60 g) tahini

3 tablespoons (48 g) mellow white miso paste

¾ teaspoon salt

1 cup (260 g) spicy salsa (see tip)

Water to thin as needed

Yield: 2 cups (about 500 g)

In a food processor, pulse the cashews until they resemble a fine crumb. Add the tahini, miso, and salt and pulse to combine. Add the salsa and purée until mostly smooth. If you'd like to thin it out, add water 1 tablespoon (15 ml) at a time until the desired consistency is reached.

TIP: Now is not the time for mild salsa. The other ingredients will mellow out the heat, so go with a medium to spicy one. A fairly runny salsa works best, but if you use a chunkier one, add water to thin as needed.

Butternut Mac & Cheese Sauce

This is the #1 recipe on my blog! Made with real whole food ingredients, this sauce shockingly resembles dairy cheese sauce. I had tried numerous plant-based mac and cheese recipes prior and none of them were worth making again. I finally stumbled upon a *VegNews* recipe that we actually liked! I made several adaptations to that recipe, made it quicker and easier, and voilà, Butternut Mac Cheese Sauce was born. This recipe is beloved by everyone from vegans to carnivores and kids to adults. Try it with pasta for a delicious creamy mac and cheese, over baked potatoes, stirred into soup, as a dip for raw or steamed vegetables, etc.

1½ cups (210 g) peeled and chopped butternut squash

½ sweet onion, diced

¼ cup (35 g) raw cashews

1 tablespoon (15 ml) fresh lemon juice

1 teaspoon salt

¼ teaspoon garlic powder

¼ teaspoon black pepper

¼ teaspoon mustard powder

⅛ teaspoon smoked paprika

⅛ teaspoon turmeric

⅛ teaspoon ground nutmeg

Yield: 2 cups (475 ml)

Add the butternut squash, onion, and cashews to a pot over high heat and cover with water by at least 1 to 2 inches (2.5 to 5 cm). Bring to a boil and then reduce the heat to low. Simmer for 15 to 20 minutes until the squash is fork tender. Reserve ¼ cup (60 ml) of the cooking liquid and drain the rest.

Add the squash mixture to a high-speed blender along with the reserved cooking liquid and the remaining ingredients. Blend until smooth.

Addictive Tofu (Two Ways)

Tofu done right is down-right addictive! Oven-baked is my go-to method because it's mostly hands off, but if you want truly crispy exteriors, panfried is the way to go!

FOR CRISPY PANFRIED TOFU:

1 package (14 ounces, or 390 g) extra-firm or super-firm tofu (not silken), drained

2 tablespoons (28 ml) peanut oil or other high-heat oil (such as coconut or avocado), divided

Salt and black pepper

FOR THE CHEWY OVEN-BAKED TOFU:

1 package (14 ounces, or 390 g) extra-firm or super-firm tofu (not silken), drained

2 tablespoons (28 ml) tamari, coconut aminos, or soy sauce (gluten-free, if desired)

1 tablespoon (15 ml) apple cider vinegar

1 tablespoon (15 ml) olive oil

1 tablespoon (20 g) pure maple syrup

1 tablespoon (15 g) Dijon mustard

Salt and black pepper

Yield: 6 servings

FOR BOTH VERSIONS

Optional: Press the tofu for 20 minutes. I find pressing extra-firm or super-firm tofu doesn't make much of a difference unless it seems very wet when it comes out of the package. If you choose to press your tofu, wrap the block of tofu in several paper towels or a clean kitchen towel and place on a plate. Place another plate on top of the tofu and weigh down the top plate. Cans or bags of beans or rice work well for this or a heavy skillet. This tower may start to topple as the tofu loses liquid, so don't use anything breakable, like glass jars, as a weight.

Cut the tofu block into bite-size cubes. You can do this however you want, but I like to stand it on end and cut it vertically in half. Lay it down and cut into fourths, turn it 90 degrees, and then cut again into fourths again.

For the Crispy Panfried Tofu: Line a large plate with a clean paper towel and set to the side.

Heat a large skillet over medium-high heat; cast-iron works best, but nonstick works, too. Add 1 tablespoon (15 ml) of peanut oil and let it heat up. Add half of the tofu cubes, spreading them out so they aren't touching; if your pan is on the smaller side, you may need to do this in three batches instead of two. If you have a splatter screen for your pan, this would be a great time to use it. If not, just be careful that you don't get splattered by the oil as it starts to pop. Cook the tofu 4 to 5 minutes on one side; do NOT move it during this time. It should flip easily when it's ready. If it's sticking when you try to flip it, let it cook another minute. I generally use kitchen tongs, but a thin flat spatula may help if you find they are sticking. Flip all the pieces over carefully and cook for another 3 to 4 minutes. You may need to adjust the heat as you go; if your pan starts to get too hot, turn it down to medium. Flip the cubes one more time and cook for another 3 to 4 minutes. Turn the tofu cubes out onto the paper towel–lined plate in one even layer to drain any excess oil. Immediately sprinkle generously with salt and pepper.

Add the remaining tablespoon (15 ml) of peanut oil to the skillet and repeat with the remaining tofu cubes.

I find 3 crispy sides is perfect, but you can certainly do all sides if you have the patience.

You can also just shake the pan each time instead of meticulously turning each one, but just know that some sides may get more done than others.

I dare you not to eat them all straight from the plate! But, if you can resist, your tofu cubes are now ready to be used in a variety of dishes.

For the Chewy Oven-Baked Tofu: Place the tofu cubes into a shallow container or bowl. Whisk together the remaining ingredients. Pour the marinade over the tofu and toss well to ensure all tofu cubes are covered. Refrigerate for 15 to 20 minutes, tossing again after 10 minutes.

Meanwhile, preheat the oven to 375°F (190°C, or gas mark 5). Line a rimmed baking sheet with parchment paper.

Remove the tofu cubes from the marinade. Place it in a single layer on the prepared baking sheet. Bake for 20 to 30 minutes, flipping every 10 minutes until golden brown, crispy on the edges, and chewy in the center.

Immediately sprinkle with salt and pepper while they're still hot.

Quick Pickled Red Onions

These pickled red onions are an easy way to add a burst of flavor to any dish. I'm not a huge fan of raw onions, but I could eat them all day like this. They're sweet and tangy, and they're the perfect complement to so many recipes.

1 large red onion, halved and sliced

½ cup (120 ml) white vinegar

½ cup (120 ml) water

2 teaspoons organic white sugar

1 teaspoon sea salt

Yield: about 2 cups (340 g)

Place the onion slices in a glass jar just large enough to hold them.

Heat the white vinegar, water, sugar, and salt over medium-high heat. Bring to a simmer and whisk until the sugar and salt are completely dissolved. This should only take a few minutes. Carefully, pour the mixture over the onions. Press the onions down into the liquid if they are sticking up. Set aside to cool.

Pickled onions will be ready to eat in about 30 minutes. The flavors will get stronger as they sit. Cover tightly and store in the refrigerator for about 1 week.

SERVING SUGGESTION: Use these pickled red onions to top sandwiches, burgers, salads, tacos, and so much more!

Acknowledgments

This book would not have been possible without the collaboration and help of so many people.

To my husband, Mike, thank you for accepting and supporting my choices from the first day I came to you with my idea to give up meat and dairy. For being open to trying new foods and flavors that you wouldn't have otherwise wanted to try. And for being there as a sounding board during all my ups and downs of not only this book, but the adventure that is being a blogger, social media influencer, and entrepreneur. I love you.

To my children, Matthew, Caroline, and Katherine, you are the reason I breathe. It was becoming a mother that changed my mindset around food and healthy living. Thank you for being my best taste testers and kitchen helpers. Thank you for your patience as I worked long hours with little time for much else. Thank you for bringing me joy and laughter every day of my life. I love you more than words can say.

To my parents, thank you for showing me that hard work and dedication always pay off. Thank you for always believing in me. Thank you for expecting me to succeed but being there to catch me if I fall. And thank you for always being willing to help with the kids when needed. I love you.

To my bestie, Paige Wulfert, thank you for always being just a phone call away. Thank you for listening to me, supporting me, believing in me, and cheering me on. You likely know more about me than any other person on this planet and I wouldn't have it any other way.

Thank you to my amazing team of recipe testers and your family and friends for your time and effort along with valuable feedback, opinions, and tips. You were incredibly helpful to me during this process. I wish I could give you all a big hug! Thank you to: Lisa Dawn Angerame, Ann Baumbach, Katie Bee, Samantha Burmeister, Michelle Lemus, Stacey Lorenz, Rachel Mersky, Lisa Prisor, and Janet Slonneger.

Thank you to my editor, Amanda Waddell, and the entire team at Fair Winds Press and The Quarto Group. It has been an amazing adventure writing this book and seeing it through to fruition. I'm so grateful for all of you and your expertise.

Last, but certainly not least, to my *Veggie Inspired* readers. I wouldn't be writing this if not for you. Thank you for your support throughout the years; for your passion and enthusiasm for my recipes; for every single one of your comments, emails, photo remakes, social media shares, and so much more. I am so lucky to be able to turn my passion for cooking into a career and will be forever grateful to all of you.

Eat Your Veggies,
Jenn

About the Author

Jenn Sebestyen is the founder, recipe developer, and photographer behind the food blog *Veggie Inspired*, which features simple and flavorful plant-based recipes. She wants to show people how easy it can be to get their daily dose of fruits and veggies in a delicious and satisfying way.

Jenn has appeared on "The Doctors" and her work has been featured in a variety of media outlets such as *Women's Health*, *Fitness*, *Self*, *Taste of Home*, *Better Homes & Gardens*, *Country Living*, *Vegan Food & Living*, *Prevention*, *Redbook*, *Buzzfeed*, *Huffington Post*, MSN, *Parade*, PETA, and many more.

She lives in Chicago with her husband and three kids where she balances being a working mom, baseball mom, softball mom, basketball mom, and football coach's wife. You can find her online at www.veggieinspired.com, on Instagram and Twitter @veggie_inspired, and on her Facebook page Veggie Inspired.

Index